RAF BOMBER COMMAND
and its aircraft 1936~1940

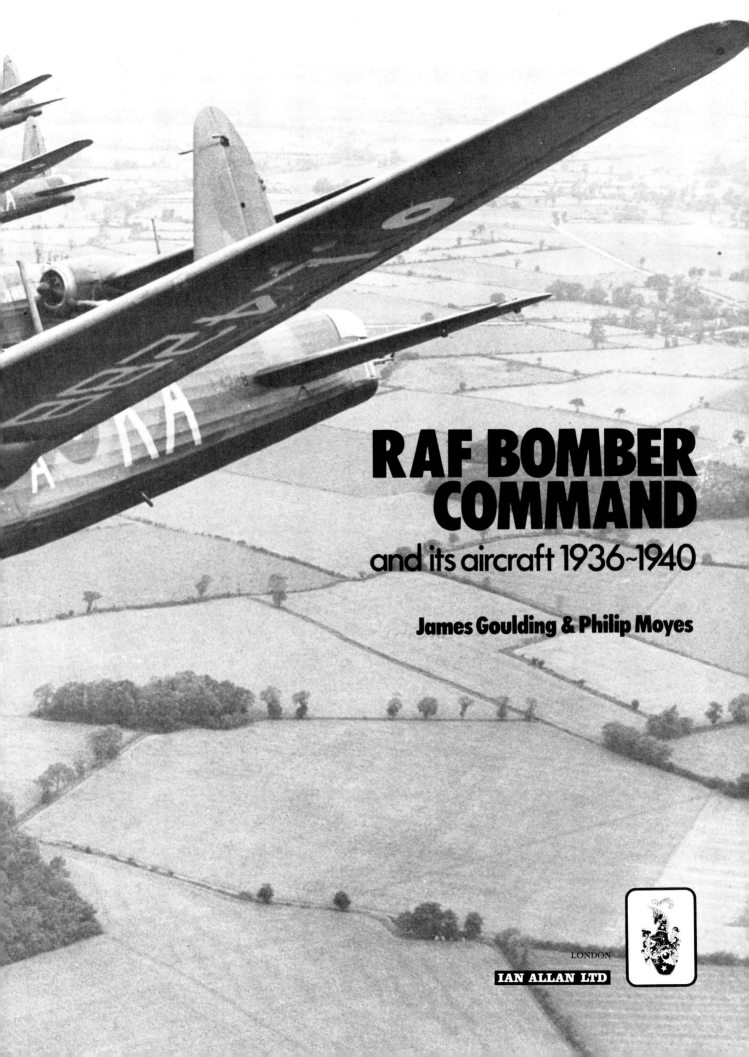

RAF BOMBER COMMAND
and its aircraft 1936~1940

James Goulding & Philip Moyes

LONDON

IAN ALLAN LTD

First published 1975
Reprinted 2002

ISBN 0 7110 0627 X

Published by Ian Allan Publishing

an imprint of Ian Allan Publishing Ltd,
Terminal House, Shepperton, Surrey TW17 8AS.
Printed by Ian Allan Printing Ltd, Hersham, Surrey
KT12 4RG.

Code: 0201/A

Contents

Colour illustrations and line drawings by James Goulding

Title page: Wellington Is of 9 Squadron, Honington, Suffolk, in the summer of 1939 shortly before the outbreak of war.

Left: Battles of 218 Squadron, AASF, pictured during the 'Phoney War'.

Preface

This book is the first of a two-volume work whose chief aim is to tell the story of RAF Bomber Command from its formation in 1936 until the end of World War II, with particular emphasis on the bombers themselves. The present volume covers the period up to the end of 1940 and describes the steps taken to forge the striking force and also how some of the first generation monoplane bombers fared in battle. To round off the story – and particularly with modellers in mind – there is a special chapter devoted to the fascinating subject of bomber camouflage and markings.

One of the prime aims of this book is to record, in unprecedented detail, the numerous little-known bomber aircraft projects of the period which never left the drawing board. It should be remembered that such design projects usually involved thousands of man hours spent in thought, discussing the drafting of layout schemes for the structure and positioning of equipment, the design of special equipment and all the many other problems associated with the first stages in the evolution of a new aeroplane. And for every project that did gain Air Ministry acceptance and eventually became actual hardware, many, many others remained firmly on paper.

It is worth mentioning, perhaps, that aeroplanes of the 'Thirties and 'Forties often bore company 'hallmarks' in the form of distinctive wing or tailplane planform, wing tip shape, fin and rudder shape, etc. Thus, for example, the Typhoon and Tornado wing and tailplane planforms can be seen in Hawker's big P.13/36 medium bomber project, typical Handley Page features are evident in the Halifax, and the Battle is obviously of Fairey origin.

It is also not out of place, perhaps, to recall that Britain's aircraft manufacturers had, by the outbreak of World War II, assembled a number of experienced and

talented design teams headed by such men as George Volkert (Handley Page), Roy Chadwick (Avro), Sydney Camm (Hawker), Rex Peirson (Vickers), Joe Smith (Supermarine), George Carter (Gloster), Marcel Lobelle (Fairey), John Lloyd (Armstrong Whitworth) and C. C. Walker and R. E. Bishop (de Havilland). Such teams ensured a constant flow of new designs and ideas, backed up by the general research work undertaken by the Royal Aircraft Establishment and other government establishments.

Possibly the most difficult task was that of selecting designs, from many with individual outstanding merit, for development into prototypes and probable production. Even after considering all the factors and ordering the building of a prototype, there was no certainty that it would behave as predicted. Fortunately, during the years covered by this volume, the cost of aircraft development was comparatively low, so it was usually possible to order prototypes of two companies' projects to meet a specific requirement and select the best for production – although in some cases, both would be adopted to ensure an adequate supply of aircraft. Thus, Bomber Command, certainly from 1941 onwards, found itself in the enviable position of having several different types of bombers which were far more potent than any used by the enemy.

G.J.G. and P.J.R.M.

ACKNOWLEDGMENTS

The authors wish to express their gratitude to the following helpers who so readily gave them their kind assistance during their search for information: Norman Barfield (BAC, Weybridge); J. M. Bruce (RAF Museum); John Gray and Peter Hayley (Hawker Siddeley Aviation, Manchester); C. H. Johns (formerly of Handley Page); E. B. Morgan (BAC, Weybridge); James Oughton (BAC, Filton); R. B. Marsh (Hawker Siddeley Aviation, Kingston); Brian Wexham (Vickers); Jim White (Shorts); and Ray Williams.

A Hampden is refuelled at a Bomber Command OTU as dusk falls./*The Aeroplane*

Introduction

The first organised British bombing raids were made in the autumn of 1914 – just a few weeks after the outbreak of World War I – by aircraft of the Royal Naval Air Service operating from Antwerp on the Belgian coast. Their weapons were 20lb Hales bombs aimed by eye from low level and their targets were German airships. Bad weather in the target areas rendered the first raids, on September 22, abortive, but in the next attack, on October 8, an airship was destroyed in its hangar at Dusseldorf.

These were the first strategic bombing attacks ever made, and thereafter the bomber element of the RNAS mainly continued in this role, a notable event during this period being the introduction, in late 1916, of the first true British heavy bomber, the famous twin-engined 0/100 biplane developed by Handley Page for the Admiralty and able to carry three quarters of a ton of bombs. The bomber element of the Royal Flying Corps confined itself, in the main, to tactical targets, one of its squadrons (No 100, formed in February 1917 and equipped with FE2B single engined 'pusher' biplanes) gaining the distinction of being the first British squadron formed specifically for night bombing.

In October 1917, as a direct result of increasing German air raids on Britain by twin-engined Gotha aeroplanes, latterly by night and in conjunction with specially-built multi-engined 'Giants' (*Riesenflugzeuge* or R-Planes), the British Government ordered the formation in France of an 'independent' strategic bombing force to bomb munition factories in the German homeland, partly in retaliation but also in the hope of breaking the deadlock which had followed the great land battles of 1916 and 1917. Named the 41st Wing and based in the Nancy area, the force was organised by General Trenchard, C-in-C of the RFC in France, and initially comprised one RNAS (Handley Page) and two RFC (single engine) squadrons. It began operations in October 1917, was expanded into the VIII Brigade in February 1918 and in June, just three

Inherited by Bomber Command on its formation in June 1936 was the sole squadron of Boulton Paul Overstrands, No 101, which received these biplane medium bombers at Bicester, Oxon, in 1935-36 and flew them until re-equipped with Bristol Blenheims in 1938. The Overstrand was the first RAF bomber to have a power-operated, enclosed gun turret mounted in the nose./ *Charles E. Brown*

8

months after the unification of the RFC and RNAS into the Royal Air Force, it was officially re-named the Independent Force; at the same time its importance was recognised by the appointment of General Trenchard himself as commander. By then negotiations were afoot to make it an interallied force by the inclusion of French, Italian and American squadrons, but subsequent events on the Western Front rendered the scheme unnecessary.

The relations of this 'independent' force with Field Marshal Haig and later with the allied generalissimo, Marshal Foch, were never precisely defined. The British Government was insistent that the operations should be independent of the commanders controlling the land campaign in France and these commanders were equally anxious that operations against the enemy should not continue regardless of the needs of the campaign. The disagreement was often sharp, so much so that at one time the British Government considered the possibility of transferring the entire force to Norfolk and using airfields in France only for refuelling. In any case the new four-engined Handley Page V/1500s which appeared in October 1918 would have operated from Norfolk had the war lasted a few days longer. (The big Handley Pages – they were partly suggested by the German 'Giants' which had been used against London – had a crew of six and a range which would have enabled them to reach Berlin with a heavy bomb load. Three of them were standing by at Bircham Newton on Armistice Day ready for such a raid.) As it was, however, this lack of precise arrangements never really mattered in practice, as the 'independent' force was invariably switched to assist the armies whenever the situation demanded, as in the German break-through in March 1918 and in the final Allied offensive in the late summer and autumn.

When the war ended in November 1918 the Independent Force had grown to 10 squadrons, four of single-engined two-seat de Havilland day bombers, five of long range twin-engined Handley Page night bombers, and one squadron of single-seat Sopwith Camel fighters which had arrived in an effort to reduce the very considerable opposition the enemy was offering to day attacks. Both in terms of numerical strength and bomb capacity the force was always too small to accomplish much, and its influence on the campaign in France was almost imperceptible. It was dispersed in the hectic demobilisation which followed the Armistice and its squadrons disbanded or, in a few cases, sent abroad on policing and airmail duties. But in 1923 when the Government realised that the post-war run-down of the RAF had gone too far and decided that provision must be made for the air defence of Britain, Sir Hugh Trenchard, by now Chief of the Air Staff, secured the inclusion of a substantial bomber element in the force to be raised.

Progress was very slow and in any case one important factor seriously reduced the value of this force for many years. In default of a clearly defined opponent, France came to be recognised as the only potential enemy who could threaten Britain by air, and the very unlikeliness of this threat took much of the urge out of bomber development. Worse still, the short distances involved if France were the enemy combined with shortage of money to stifle the quest for range – always an expensive item. Only by depriving itself of several badly needed items, such as accommodation, was the RAF able to afford new aircraft, but even then orders were necessarily small and had to be spread thinly among the 'family' firms in the aircraft industry in order to keep them alive. Most of these firms were mainly establishments for research and development in those days and it is of interest to note that the only really significant advance in bomber development at that time was a private venture, ie the two-seat Fairey Fox of 1925 which advanced the speed of day bombers by 50mph, enabling it to outpace any fighter in service.

In July 1934, when German rearmament and the collapse of the League of Nations Disarmament Conference finally resulted in the signal being given for the expansion of the RAF, the UK-based bomber force then comprised 28 squadrons organised in the 'Western Area' and the 'Central Area' of the Air Defence of Great Britain. Most of them were light bomber units and apart from those at Bircham Newton in Norfolk, they were all based in the counties of Wiltshire, Hampshire, Berkshire and Oxfordshire – a disposition based on the aforementioned assumption that any air attack on Britain in a European war could only be made by France. At this stage the force was still made up of biplanes with poor speeds, short ranges and modest bomb loads. Newest and most potent type was the twin-engined Handley Page Heyford with a crew of 4, three guns, a range out-and-home of 920 miles with a 1 600lb bomb load and a top speed of 142mph; but although it had entered service as recently as November 1933 it too had been rendered obsolete by the new all-metal multi-engined Dornier 23 and Junkers 52/3m monoplanes which were now coming into use with Hitler's clandestine *Luftwaffe*.

The rest of the home defence bomber force's aircraft

Above right: Included in this unique view of the New Types Park at the 1936 RAF Display at Hendon are the prototypes of the five key types in Bomber Command's pre-war expansion programme – the Fairey Battle (exhibit number 4), Vickers B.9/32 (7), AW Whitley (9), HP Hampden (8) and Bristol 142 (5), which latter was the immediate precursor of the Blenheim/*The Aeroplane*

Right: In October 1937 'top brass' of the Luftwaffe – the very armed force against whose potential threat Britain was rearming – were allowed to visit several RAF stations in this country as a goodwill gesture by the British Government. The photograph shows the German mission and their escort inspecting a Handley Page Harrow at Mildenhall. General Milch is in front with Air Chief Marshal Sir Edgar Ludlow-Hewitt, AOC-in-C Bomber Command, followed by General Stumpff and AVM P. H. L. Playfair, AOC 3 Group.

were also biplanes and varied from the lumbering Vickers Virginia – the Heyford's main partner in the night bomber squadrons – to the relatively nimble Hawker Hart single-engined two-seat light day bomber. Like the Heyford, all had the same basic armament as their World War I predecessors, ie fixed and/or moveable .303in machine guns, and the pilots did their own navigating. Nevertheless, several new types were gradually being developed, the best of these – but still on paper – being the prototypes of what was to become the famous trio of heavies which formed the backbone of Bomber Command in the early part of World War II, the Armstrong Whitworth Whitley, Handley Page Hampden and Vickers Wellington.

Expansion of the RAF after the alarm bells rang was programmed in several successive schemes, each representing a re-think about future requirements in the light of changing circumstances and in every case never fully implemented. The first scheme – Scheme 'A' – was announced in July 1934 and aimed at boosting first-line strength in order to impress Hitler, albeit at the expense of reserves. Insofar as the bomber force went, the aim was to expand it over the five-year period ending March 31, 1939, to reach 41 squadrons, 22 of which were to be light bombers, of little use in any attack on Germany, yet relatively cheap and having the further advantage of enabling more pilots to be trained operationally. Another reason for opting for so many light bombers was that no satisfactory medium or heavy bomber had yet been put into production. The Government disliked this move, but it was the only choice if expansion were to proceed and a 'deterrent' created. Apart from this initial sacrifice of quality for quantity the expansion of the force was guided by

sound principles, and wise decisions were taken which were to create a striking force with a hitting power at least as great as Germany's – and ultimately far greater.

A full account of the Expansion Programme is outside the scope of this book, and in any case it has been fully covered in the Official Histories, but nevertheless mention must be made here of Scheme 'F'. This was announced in February 1936 and made provision, among other things, for a vast increase in the RAF's striking power by replacing light bombers with mediums and the creation of much larger reserves, all within three years. Again, this was a move in the right direction; but the aircraft industry, adapting itself to the radical change from biplane to monoplane and from fabric covered to stressed metal-covered construction, simply could not cope with the workload that Scheme 'F' entailed. The industry's problems were indeed enormous: in order to produce the highly sophisticated and complex modern aircraft, factories had to be reorganised, stocks of raw materials changed, workers trained for new tasks, and time-honoured hand-made methods of small run production replaced by jig, tool and assembly line methods of quantity production.

To save the situation, Lord Swinton, in April 1936, instituted the Shadow Factory Scheme which, initially, was a means of utilising the resources of the motor vehicle industry to provide extra production capacity. This involved the building of new State-owned aero-engine and airframe component and assembly plants which were equipped and run by such leading motor firms as Austin, Daimler, Rootes and Standard, and which turned out products designed by some 'parent' firm within the aircraft industry. This scheme, which

soon got under way, was supplemented early in 1938 by a further shadow scheme which provided for the erection of State-owned factories which were to be managed by approved firms in the aircraft industry to increase production.

On June 18, 1936, the Air Council abolished the Air Defence of Great Britain and reorganised it into two separate commands, Bomber and Fighter, each with its own Air Officer Commander-in-Chief who was directly responsible to the Air Council. At the time, these moves were undoubtedly fully justified, and indeed if the decision had not been taken to concentrate Fighter Command on the task of defending Britain against air attack, it might well have cost the nation defeat in 1940. However, the new set-up did also have grave drawbacks: the gulf between attack and defence was widened, combined operations were rendered more difficult, and joint tactical planning was neglected. Theoretically, the Chief of the Air Staff should have remedied any such defects, but in practice his many other duties often precluded this, and the strategic offensive suffered accordingly.

Also formed on June 18, 1936, were Coastal Command – by reorganising the former Coastal Area – and Training Command, which latter, with few exceptions, took control of all training units in the United Kingdom.

Bomber Command had its headquarters at Uxbridge and initially comprised four groups, Nos 1, 2, 3 and 6, the last being an Auxiliary group. It began life equipped entirely with biplanes, chiefly the previously-mentioned Virginia and Heyford heavy night bombers and Hart light day bombers, but the Harts were soon replaced by the new, marginally faster, Hind which

also equipped the new light bomber squadrons which mushroomed throughout the command during 1936-37.

Some of the old 'heavies' lingered on until mid-1939, but meanwhile, in November 1936, came the delivery of the first Fairey Hendon to 38 Squadron at Marham, an event which heralded the advent of the modern monoplane bomber. Classed as a long-range night bomber, the Hendon had been put into production during the early expansion period before the Air Council knew exactly what kind of bombing force it wanted to make. Consequently it became regarded as an interim type – one of several such products of this era, all of whose beginnings will presently be fully described, together with those of their much improved successors.

To accommodate the expanding bomber force, a chain of new bases was built in eastern England and in 1937 the first concrete runways were laid; by the outbreak of war, however, the majority of bomber airfields were still all-grass.

The training of crews was hampered by the fact that the new all-metal monoplanes were vastly more com-

Below left: For a long time after World War I the RAF's bomber arm had to make do with long-obsolete aircraft and weapons and even the bombs of later vintage used in World War II were, more often than not, inferior to their German counterparts. Here, in the early 1930s, armourers prepare crude WWI-type 115lb bombs for loading onto Vickers Virginia X night bombers, which were the final development of the original 'Ginnie' of 1922.

Below: Playing a key role in the RAF Expansion Scheme was the Hawker Hind light day bomber which, because it was cheap and simple to produce, enabled many new pilots to be trained operationally in readiness for the modern all-metal monoplane bombers which were to follow. Shown are Hinds of 44 Squadron.

plex than their lumbering predecessors, introducing, as standard, such items as constant-speed propellers, automatic pilots, retractable undercarriages and power-operated turrets. In the new big bombers, such as the Hampden, Whitley and Wellington, navigation became the duty of a specialist crew member although, as the Air Council still imagined that in the event of war the Hampden and Wellington would be able to operate with impunity by day, night flying and its many hidden problems was largely overlooked in the training curriculum. Such exercises as did take place, notably the Annual Air Defence Exercises held in the late summer, were thoroughly unrealistic; for no one really appreciated the immense problems that would have to be surmounted by any 'shooting war' before a sizeable force of bombers could reach its target, let alone identify it positively and do any worthwhile damage.

Left: Ancient and modern. Lumbering, 108mph Vickers Virginia Xs, of the type that remained in first-line service until as late as 1937 make a sharp contrast with the sleek, 254mph Handley Page Hampdens (*lower photo*) representing the first generation of new monoplane bombers which entered service in the late 'Thirties as the RAF was urgently re-armed./*Top photo by Charles E. Brown*

Below: Noteworthy as the first all-metal low wing cantilever monoplane to enter RAF squadron service was then ultra-modern looking Fairey Hendon night bomber which briefly formed the equipment of 38 Squadron, one flight of which was for a time detached to form the nucleus of the new 115 Squadron. K5085, seen here, was the first of the 14 production Hendons./*Charles E. Brown*

The strength and character of Germany's air and ground defences was equally unknown, but on the other hand British Intelligence did glean a reasonably accurate picture of potential targets vital to a German war effort. As a result the Air Council drew up thirteen directives known as Western Air Plans which were approved on October 1, 1937, and covered such a wide range of options as a major air strike on the *Luftwaffe's* bomber force, an attack on industrial targets in the Ruhr, Rhineland and Saar – particularly oil targets – and raids on enemy naval vessels at sea.

As time and experience showed, many of the Western Air Plans were extremely far-sighted insofar as they gave Bomber Command a remarkable strategic insight for a major bombing offensive. Unfortunately, they also contained an element of blind faith in the ability of Bomber Command – faith which stemmed from the success of the Gotha raids of 1917/18 on London, the *Luftwaffe* raids on Spanish towns during the civil war, and the unrealistic air defence exercises which have just been mentioned. Had Britain and her ally, France, adopted an offensive policy at the outset of World War II, the history of Bomber Command – and indeed the entire war – almost certainly would have been very different. But fortunately the Allies adopted a defensive strategy thus enabling Bomber Command to conserve its aircrews and simultaneously reinforce them in number in readiness for the advent of the four-engined heavies on which rested the only hope of making good a major bombing offensive.

Re-equipment in Prospect

Development of the Handley Page Hampden and Vickers Wellington prototypes (to Specification B.9/32), Fairey Battle (to P.27/32) and the Hawker Hart replacement (to P.4/34).

Bomber Command entered World War II armed with five main types of monoplane bombers, the Wellington, Whitley, Hampden, Battle and Blenheim. The design histories of these aircraft, however, began before the formation of Bomber Command, during the years 1932-1934.

At this time the RAF's home-based bomber element was equipped with three categories of aircraft – the fast light day bomber, the larger twin-engined day bomber, and the long-range night bomber. Squadrons available consisted of a number armed with small light bombers, one operating the Boulton Paul Sidestrand twin-engined medium day bomber, and several operating large night bombers.

In 1932 the majority of night bombing squadrons operated the Vickers Virginia, with the Handley Page Heyford entering service the following year. Another B.19/27 design, the Fairey Hendon, the first of the

bomber monoplanes, was on order and at first expected to become the main replacement for the Vickers Virginia. Although the Air Staff had previously been reticent about adopting the monoplane their uncertainties and prejudice had by now been overcome, and the very big Fairey night bomber had won the B.19/27 competition as the new standard night bomber. Fourteen had initially been ordered, with a further 60 to follow. The Handley Page Heyford had also been ordered as an insurance against any problems with the Hendon.

Unfortunately, the loss of valuable Hendon test flying time, due to the crash of the prototype and problems with production, caused such a delay in getting the aircraft into service that the second order was cancelled. The Hendon did not enter service until the end of 1936, and then only fully equipped one squadron, No 38. The Heyford was therefore produced in greater numbers than had originally been planned, and the Virginia continued to give faithful service long after it was due for replacement.

All the bomber squadrons were urgently in need of new monoplane designs to keep in pace with developments abroad. Monoplane bombers were either in service, or flying in prototype form, in many countries. France had the Bloch 200 and 210, the Potez 54 and Amiot 140. Germany was flying the Dornier Do 23 and Junkers Ju 52/3m in secret, flouting Versailles Peace Treaty obligations. Italy had developed the Savoia-Marchetti 81 and Caproni 101. Russia had built up considerable experience of operating monoplanes with the ANT-1 and ANT-6 twin- and four-engined bombers in what was then the biggest strategic bomber force in the world.

In America advanced all-metal monoplane bomber designs were under development, including the Boeing B-9 and Martin B-10. A further significantly advanced aeroplane was the Douglas DC-1 commercial transport monoplane.

The RAF's immediate needs in the bomber field concerned development of a Sidestrand successor and a replacement type for the existing generation of heavy night bombers. It was realised that some years would elapse before such aircraft could be brought into service.

In 1932 the first steps were taken towards the issue of a specification for the development of a new twin-engined day bomber, Specification B.9/32. Originally this called for a bomb load equal to 1lb per horsepower, made up with 112lb, 120lb, 250lb, 450lb, or 500lb

bombs. Provision was to be made to carry at least 4 x 20lb or the normal bomb load weight made up with 20lb bombs, or as many as possible. Range was to be 600 miles at full cruise throttle setting at 15,000ft, plus half an hour at ground level at full throttle. Tankage was to be sufficient to permit extra fuel to be carried equal to 50 per cent of the bomb load.

The aircraft was to have good manoeuvrability, a requirement inherited from the Sidestrand, and a good view for formation flying, for bombing and night landing. Adequate navigational facilities were to be provided, and a crew of four carried.

Boulton Paul Sidestrands of 101 Squadron, the sole squadron thus armed. The Sidestrand was the predecessor of the Overstrand illustrated on page 8. /*Bristol Aeroplane Co*

A speed of not less than 190mph at some height between 10,000ft and 15,000ft was required. Service ceiling was not to be less than 22,000ft and the landing speed not over 60mph.

After discussions, changes to the B.9/32 specification were made. The wing span was limited to not more than 70ft. The aircraft was to carry a pilot, navigator, W/T operator and one gunner, bomb aiming and other gunner's duties being performed as required by the navigator and W/T operator.

The bomb load was specified in more detail as being the following loads: As many 20lb bombs as possible, 10 x 112lb, 10 x 120lb GP (General Purpose), 6 x 250lb GP, SAP (Semi-Armour-Piercing) or AS (Anti-Submarine), 3 x 450lb AP (Armour Piercing), 3 x 500lb GP or SAP, 3 x 520lb, 3 x 550lb, 1 x 1,100lb 'B', or 1 x 1,500lb. At a later date the two last bomb types were deleted from the specification.

It was stipulated that there should be one nose gun position, and two aft of the wing. The specification stated 'each cockpit is to be properly screened from the wind. Particular attention is to be given to protecting the aft gunners: with this object in view the fuselage is to be designed to deflect the air flow from the region of each rear cockpit (gunner's position) to an extent which will enable the gunners to operate the guns over their entire fields of fire without appreciable effort.'

The fuel tanks permanently included in the fuel system were to be large enough in the aggregate to hold 73 gallons of fuel more than would be necessary for a range of 600 miles, plus the quantity required for half an hour with the engines developing the maximum power permissible at ground level. Auxiliary tanks were to be provided to increase the range to 1,250 miles at 15,000ft cruising at 125mph.

Speed and service ceiling were unchanged from the original specification, but the landing speed was required to be not more than 65mph, but 60mph if possible.

The specification was sent out to a number of companies, with the invitation to submit designs for tender.

Two designs were to be selected from those submitted, for prototype development and probable production.

In 1932 the Geneva Disarmament Conference was opened under the auspices of the League of Nations. The World Powers had earlier failed to agree on total disarmament, and this conference had been convened to seek agreement on armament limitation. A major proposal, with which the British Government was in full agreement, was that the tare or empty weight of bomber aircraft should not exceed 3 metric tons – approximately 6,300lb. This caused considerable argument and discussion which extended over some two years. A number of countries, including Japan, refused to agree to such a proposal and made known their intention of ignoring such a limitation if it became accepted.

The Geneva Conference weight limitation proposal placed the Air Staff in a difficult position with regard to the Sidestrand replacement twin-engined day bomber. The tare weight limitation was recognised as being a serious restriction on designers; it inevitably limited the weight and power of the engines to be used – which in turn meant a very light basic structure. If the Air Staff ignored the tare weight limitation and produced the future bomber in the form they wanted, and got it into squadron service in numbers, there was the possibility, in the event of a world agreement on bomber weight, of having to scrap the RAF's main day bomber force virtually overnight. It thus seemed advisable to add a tare weight limitation of 6,300lb to the B.9/32 specification, and see what designs could be produced in this form. This was later raised to 6,500lb because it was felt that certain items in the aircraft

Last of the RAF's biplane heavy bombers, the Handley Page Heyford entered service in November 1933 and remained in front-line use for over five years, being superseded by the new monoplane bombers of the Expansion era – notably Whitleys and Wellingtons. This Heyford, a Mk III, sports on its wheel fairings, the nocturnal bat badge of 9 Squadron and the picture shows how the engine cowling side panels hinged down to provide working platforms for the fitters.

could be considered as part of the military load, although they were originally quoted in the tare weight figures. It was hoped that this would make things a little easier for designers.

In order to save weight designers chose medium-powered engines, the Rolls-Royce Goshawk and the Bristol Mercury being the most favoured. At this time the Goshawk promised much for the future, having a low weight for its power rating. Unfortunately, its early promise was not to be fulfilled, due to the over-elaborate evaporative cooling system.

A number of B.9/32 projects were submitted, including a Sidestrand development from Boulton Paul. The two most promising designs came from Handley Page and Vickers: the Handley Page design was a Goshawk powered mid-wing monoplane, while the Vickers bomber was powered by either Goshawks or Mercuries and of high wing layout. Both companies, however, were having much difficulty in keeping to the 6,500lb tare weight limit. It was proving extremely difficult for them to achieve the specified performance figures on the engine power, and the engine power and size could not be increased because of the tare weight limit.

The Air Staff, deeply conscious of the design problem and reluctant to have the new day bomber compromised by the restriction, were in a quandary. The disarmament talks at Geneva between the World Powers became so protracted and unpromising that the Air Staff moved increasingly towards ignoring the tare weight limitation and permitting the designers to choose higher-powered engines in order to achieve the specification requirements. But always there was the possibility of an international agreement being signed which could render the future bomber force illegal. It was, however, considered unlikely that governments would have to scrap their bomber forces at once, and it was likely that such an order would take some years to carry out. It therefore seemed to be a justifiable risk to permit the tare weight of the Sidestrand replacement twin-engined bombers to rise above the Geneva limit, because the types could probably serve for a few years even if an agreement was signed.

Handley Page and Vickers were selected to proceed with their designs, with the Air Ministry and Air Staff turning a blind eye to modest increases over the 6,500lb tare weight limit. The designers were, however, still required to keep a strict eye on tare weight, which meant continuing with the Goshawk and Mercury engines for the time being, but using the highest-powered versions of these engines irrespective of weight.

While work on these types continued, the Air Staff considered that it would be prudent to develop another Sidestrand replacement designed strictly within the Geneva Convention 3 ton tare weight limit, and to order a substantial number of this type. This would ensure that in the event of a world agreement being signed, the day bomber squadrons would still have a modern monoplane of the largest size permitted. This new bomber would have a similar bomb load and range to the B.9/32, but would be powered by a single high-rated engine. The tare weight would be lighter due to the reduced defensive armament and use of a single engine. The requirements were set out in Specification P.27/32, and design tenders were invited from a number of companies including Fairey, Armstrong Whitworth, Bristol and Hawker.

On June 7, 1934, the Chief of the Air Staff decided that the tare weight limitation should be removed from the two B.9/32 projects, and letters to this effect were sent to Handley Page and Vickers on June 13. The Geneva Conference was unlikely ever to agree to the disarmament proposals in any form, and much time had already been lost in trying to comply with the limit. Handley Page and Vickers set about the task of redesigning their projects without any tare weight limitation, and in August 1934 they both requested permission to re-engine the B.9/32s with either Bristol Pegasus air-cooled radials or Bristol Perseus sleeve-valve radials. The Air Ministry granted this request on August 21. On August 15 the range of the B.9/32s was increased to 1,500 miles. The tare weight limitation of 6,500lb was formally removed from the specification on June 21, 1934.

Handley Page's B.9/32 design complied closely with the specification in two particular respects: its wing span of 69ft 4in was close to the requirement that the span should not be more than 70ft, and the unique thin, boom-like rear fuselage gave built-in protection against the air flow for the two rear gunners. The very narrow rear fuselage had previously been used in the Handley Page experimental general-purpose monoplane.

The new bomber used a mid-wing layout, with the area beneath the wing spars free from structural members to provide good stowage for the bomb load. Twin fins and rudders were used on the tail unit to give unobstructed fields of fire to rearward. The wing was equipped with slats, which gave the aircraft very docile behaviour at the stall and permitted landing speeds of about 60mph. The first prototype of Handley Page's B.9/32, known by the works number HP52, was powered by two Bristol Pegasus PE 5S(a) engines, which gave it a top speed of about 265mph – well above the specification speed requirement. The rear gun positions each housed a single Lewis gun: the upper gunner was given additional wind shielding with a folding Perspex cover, while the lower gunner was housed at first in a modified Heyford 'dustbin' turret faired into the fuselage contours. (This latter item was altered after flight trials to a fixed, smooth contour, with an opening for the Lewis gun). The prototype HP52 had a temporary, angular Perspex nose turret position, which was intended to eventually house one Lewis gun on a moving mounting. The overall length of the HP52 was 52ft 5in.

The prototype, K4240, was completed in June 1936

and made its first flight on June 21, from Radlett, with Major J. L. H. B. Cordes at the controls. At the time it was one of the most advanced twin-engined bombers in existence, and in August 1936 an initial production order was placed for 180 HP52s, designated Hampden I to Specification 30/36. Another contract for 100 of these new bombers was placed with Short Brothers and Harland at Belfast. These were to be powered by two Napier Dagger 24-cylinder air-cooled engines, and would enter service under the type name Hereford I. The second prototype HP52, L7271, was completed early in 1937 and differed from the first prototype in having a less angular Perspex front fuselage section, contoured to match an intended front turret of similar type to that used on the Handley Page Harrow. After criticism of the navigator's compartment on the prototypes, the front turret was discarded in favour of a smooth Perspex streamlined nose on the production type, which was to house the navigator and bomb aimer. L7271 served, after conversion to Napier Dagger engines, as the Hereford prototype, in which form it made its first flight on July 1, 1937. K4240 was painted in what is best described as a greenish khaki shade. L7271 was at first left in natural metal finish, but was later sprayed overall in Aluminium (silver). The HP52 carried a maximum bomb load of 3,500lb and was an aircraft of outstanding agility.

After the decision to change over to Bristol Pegasus engines, the Vickers B.9/32 design was completely re-shaped. From a high-wing monoplane layout, the new design changed to that of a very elegant mid-wing monoplane with a single fin and rudder. In order to maintain a tight control on the tare weight it was considered that Barnes Wallis' geodetic structural system could offer big advantages over a more orthodox structure. The geodetic system, developed originally as a method of achieving extreme lightness in the airship *R.100*, had already been successfully applied to the Vickers G.4/31 biplane and monoplane. The G.4/31 biplane used the structure only in the fuselage, but Vickers' private venture G.4/31 monoplane extended the system to the entire airframe.

The fuselage form of the B.9/32 was beautifully contoured, not only for aerodynamic reasons but also to achieve perfect stress paths for the criss-cross metal structural members. (Further research proved that the near-perfect elliptical cross-section of the fuselage was not necessary to achieve strength, and the production-type cross-section was modified to permit a greater bomb bay volume and to accommodate other operational features.) The entire geodetic structure was fabric-covered, which was, in some ways, a retrograde feature, but it later did prove to have advantages – notably ease of repairing minor surface damage.

Below: The Handley Page HP 52, B.9/32, twin-engine day bomber. This aircraft formed the basis for the Handley Page Hampden twin-engined day bomber for the Royal Air Force. The Handley Page HP52 1st prototype, K4240 (*lower left*) and the Handley Page HP52 2nd prototype, L7271 (*lower right*) are also shown.

Right: The first prototype HP 52 Hampden, K4240. Note the angular crew station transparencies and the small mainwheels. It is quite understandable, upon studying these pictures, how the Hampden came to earn such nicknames in the RAF as the 'Flying Suitcase', 'Flying Panhandle' and 'Flying Tadpole'.

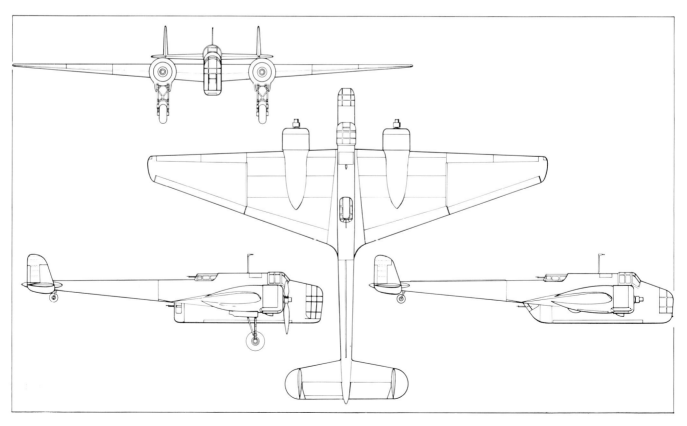

A rotating nose cupola, contoured to the fine fuselage lines, housed one Lewis gun on a manually-operated mounting, and a similar Lewis gun mounting was housed in the extreme tail. The tail cupola formed part of the locally fattened rear fuselage. The peculiar shape of the rear fuselage was apparently determined by the theory that a lighter structure would result from streamlining the main fuselage down to the tail unit and then bulging out the gunner's compartment, rather than streamlining the fuselage contour down to the extreme end of the cupola in a smooth curve, with a consequently deeper rear fuselage. Another Lewis gun, also on a manually-operated mounting, was in a mid-upper position with a retracting glazed cover. The glazing of the pilot's compartment was mainly of flat panelling, which looked rather out of place on such a perfect fuselage form and which was severely criticised during test flying because of sunlight glare reflecting from the flat panels.

The high-aspect ratio wing, with slight double taper, measured 85ft 10in in span but although this was well over the specification limit of 70ft this was accepted by the Air Ministry in the interests of aerodynamic efficiency. The overall length of the B.9/32 was 60ft 6in. The bomber was powered by two Bristol Pegasus PE5SM engines, which gave it a maximum speed of 250mph at 8,000ft at a weight of 21,000lb. Its tare weight at this stage had risen to 11,508lb, nearly double the original specification limit.

As completed the Vickers B.9/32 was a far more effective and potent bomber than could ever have been achieved if the tare weight restrictions had remained. It could carry three extra 250lb bombs, making nine in all, and no less than six extra 500lb bombs, totalling nine in the full load – well over the specification requirement. Its ferry range was 3,200 miles at 213mph without bomb load – more than double the range required in the specification. Maximum range with bomb load was 1,500 miles.

By the early summer of 1936 the Vickers B.9/32, K4049, was complete and on June 15 it made its maiden flight in the hands of 'Mutt' Summers, Vickers-Armstrong's chief test pilot. It was flown from Brooklands, the aerodrome in the middle of the racing circuit that was witness to so many first flights of Vickers and Hawker aeroplanes.

At first the name Crecy was given to the bomber but in September 1936, shortly after an initial order for 180 production models had been placed, the name was changed to Wellington. The initial order was placed in June, before the first meeting to decide the details of the first production model, the Wellington I, which latter was eventually built to Specification 29/36 issued in February 1937.

Successful test flying of the Vickers B.9/32 continued throughout 1936 and into 1937, with the aircraft showing excellent qualities and much promise, but during Service tests in April 1937 it was totally destroyed. A failure of the elevator horn balance caused the aircraft to flip over onto its back in a dive from which it could not recover. The pilot was thrown out through the cockpit canopy and escaped by parachute, but his observer was killed. The accident to the prototype did not affect the Wellington I production programme because K4049 bore little resemblance to the Wellington I, whose design had now been finalised. Work went steadily ahead as the months went by and at the end of 1937 the first Wellington I was ready for trials.

While the replacement of the Sidestrand was being planned, the Air Staff also considered what type of aeroplane should replace the single-engined light bombers, principally the Hawker Hart. After dis-

The Vickers B.9/32, prototype of the Wellington, takes off from Brooklands on a test flight. Profile shape of the Vickers-Supermarine Stranraer flying boat was borrowed for this aircraft to reduce design time.

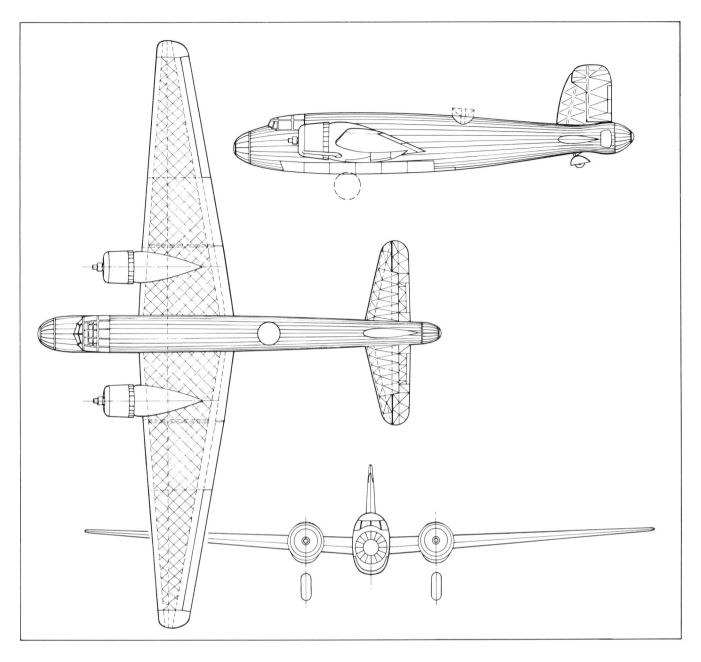

cussions it was thought that the replacement bomber should have a single engine, carry a crew of two, carry 1,000lb of bombs over 600 miles, and have a speed of not less than 195mph. For protection this bomber would have one moveable rear Lewis gun for the observer and a fixed Vickers gun for the pilot.

It was obvious that such a bomber was going to be considerably larger than existing light bomber types and, apart from the number of engines, was similar to the twin-engined Sidestrand replacement in general performance, range and bomb load. The tare weight limitation was at the time still causing doubts about the final acceptance of the twin-engined Sidestrand replacement, and it therefore became necessary to consider adopting another lighter type that did conform to the 6,300lb tare weight limitation. The Air Staff decided that the best solution would be to order two single-engined bombers – one a Sidestrand replacement

The Vickers Type 271, B.9/32, day bomber, powered by two Bristol Pegasus X engines. The prototype, K4049, had a comparatively short test flying life before it was destroyed, but it provided sufficient data to prove the soundness of the design as the basis for a production twin-engined day bomber for Bomber Command. The Wellington bore little resemblance to the B.9/32 structurally, but the two were sufficiently close in wing area, wing and tailplane planform and nacelle position to give a good indication of the Wellington's characteristics.

with a tare weight limitation of 6,300lb, designed to Specification P.27/32, and the second a true Hawker Hart replacement light fighter-bomber, of small size and carrying a normal bomb load of half that of the P.27/32, designed to Specification P.4/34.

Specification P.27/32 was issued to the aircraft industry in its finalised form as a requirement for a single-engined landplane for day bombing carrying a crew of two and having a tare weight limitation of 6,300lb. The required bomb load was as follows: 8 x 20lb, 8 x 50lb, 8 x 100lb, 8 x 112lb, 8 x 120lb, 4 x 250lb, or 2 x 500 lb – a total load of 1,000lb. The normal range with 1,000lb of bombs, which was originally 600 miles, was increased to 720 miles. Range with auxiliary tanks was 1,500 miles at 15,000ft at a cruising speed of 125mph. The maximum speed remained not less than 195mph. The P.27/32 had to be capable of certain aerobatics, notably loop, slow roll, half loop and roll off the top and vertical banked turns. Armament remained light, one moveable gun for the second crew member and a fixed gun for the pilot. As will be seen, the P.27/32 day bomber was to be similar to the B.9/32 in performance, load-carrying ability and range, but was single-engined and strictly limited in tare weight.

When the P.27/32 specification was first drafted it was envisaged that the new bomber could be powered by the military, production version of the Rolls-Royce 'R' racing engine, the Rolls-Royce Griffon. It has often been quoted that the Merlin engine was a production development of the racing engine, but this is only partially true. It may also be surprising to learn that the Griffon engine existed, at least on paper, as long ago as 1932 in view of the fact that it was not used operationally until later in the war years. The Griffon engine was in most respects, certainly dimensionally, the production version of the 'R' engine. The Rolls-Royce Merlin was in many ways a scaled-down version of the Griffon, principally for installation in single-seat fighters. Because of this, and its importance in other new aircraft types, most of the development by Rolls-Royce during the immediate pre-war years was put into the Merlin, with Griffon development taking second place. The bigger engine therefore had a longer gestation period. Fortunately, the Griffon engine was not substantially bigger than the Merlin in overall dimensions, which made its installation in existing fighters possible.

When the P.27/32 bomber was under consideration, future areas of conflict were not defined and war with France, or against any enemy on the Continent immediately opposite the East coast of Britain was a possibility. The increase in range in the revised specification brought Paris within range of Home Defence squadrons equipped with the new bomber based on airfields in southern England.

Four companies tendered designs for the new bomber, Fairey, Armstrong Whitworth, Bristol and Hawker.

Hawker's design was a typical product of that company, intended to be built of a tubular steel and duralumin structure covered in fabric. The forward part of the fuselage was to be covered in polished metal. The bomber was to be powered by either the Rolls-Royce Merlin engine or Bristol Hydra radial engine. The cockpits for the pilot and rear gunner were open, the gunner having a folding windshield. Two 500lb bombs were carried in the fuselage beneath the low

mid-wing spar. The undercarriage retracted into bulges under the wing, with part of the wheel protruding. A single Lewis gun was provided for the rear gunner and the pilot had a single Vickers gun mounted alongside his cockpit. All-up weights of the Merlin and Hydra versions were 8,162lb and 8,113lb respectively.

Armstrong Whitworth's AW29 was a typical John Lloyd design, angular and functional. It was powered by the Armstrong Siddeley Tiger 14-cylinder air-cooled radial engine of 880hp, but another version was proposed with the Armstrong Siddeley Deerhound engine. The wing was broad in chord and very thick in root section, tapering in both plan and head-on thickness considerably to the tip. The bomb load was housed in the thick wing, and it normally consisted of four 250lb bombs. Rear defence was provided by a single Lewis gun in an enclosed rotating turret, manually-operated. The pilot operated a fixed Vickers or Browning gun. A single fin and rudder design was used for the tail unit, and the undercarriage retracted backwards to lie in the wing with the wheels partially exposed. Construction of this rugged aircraft was mainly of metal, although the aft part of the wing and control surfaces were fabric covered over a light metal structure.

Only one AW29 (K4299) was built and because of priority given to two other AW designs, the Whitley bomber and the Ensign airliner, its construction was delayed. The first flight eventually took place from Baginton on December 6, 1939, with AW's chief test pilot C. K. Turner-Hughes at the controls, but not long afterwards the AW29 was damaged in a forced belly-landing and it never flew again. Estimated top speed of the AW29 was 225mph at 17,700ft while the range was quoted as 685 miles.

The first design by Fairey to meet the requirements of P.27/32 was accepted and received a contract for a prototype to be delivered by September 1935. During 1934 Fairey's chief engineer and chief designer, Marcel Lobelle, headed a party which toured centres of aviation in America. At this time a number of new all-metal aeroplanes of advanced design were under development in America and both the Air Ministry and the British aircraft industry were interested in obtaining any information and ideas on new structural and aerodynamic techniques to ensure that the new prototypes being developed for the expansion of the RAF were in the forefront of world aviation developments.

Above right: Armstrong Whitworth's prototype built to meet the Air Ministry's P.27/32 day bomber specification, the AW 29. Before it was eventually scrapped, some work was done towards adapting it to serve as a test-bed for the new AS Deerhound engine, but a change of plan led to the Whitley being used for this purpose instead.

Right: By far the most elegant and technically advanced of the P.27/32 prototypes was the Fairey aircraft, K4303, prototype of the Battle, shown here in flight at Fairey's Great West Aerodrome (now part of Heathrow Airport) in March 1936.

After the return to this country of Fairey's technical team, its P.27/32 bomber was completely redesigned in the light of new information and the revised bomber was much improved in both structure and aerodynamic form. On October 18, 1934, C. R. Fairey wrote to the Director of Contracts at the Air Ministry informing him of the redesign of the P.27/32 giving details of its greatly improved performance and requesting an extension of the delivery date to December 1935. The Director of Contracts agreed to the later date in view of the improved aircraft that would result.

Fairey's revised P.27/32 was typical of the elegant aeroplanes designed under the guidance of Marcel Lobelle, and by far the most advanced in structural design and performance. The new aircraft was powered by a Rolls-Royce Merlin engine and was an all-metal monoplane of 54ft wing span. The overall length was 42ft 1¾in. The wing, of all-metal construction, had a thick root section tapering to a thin tip section, and the main bomb load of four 250lb bombs was housed in separate wing cells. An additional cell was provided for lighter bombs. The main undercarriage units retracted backwards to lie horizontal in the wing, leaving the wheels partially protruding from the undersurface. The airflow behind the exposed wheels was smoothed by fixed fairings.

In order to counteract torque at cruising and higher speeds without the need for trimming, the fin and rudder unit was offset and had a cambered aerofoil section.

The crew of two were housed beneath a continuous glazed canopy. The pilot's hood was designed to slide backwards, and the gunner was given protection from the airflow when operating his gun by a folding portion of the long canopy, which formed a windshield. The rear Lewis gun was mounted on a special Fairey-designed retractable mounting attached to a rotating cone, which also formed part of the rear canopy fairing. The pilot operated a single fixed Vickers or Browning .303in gun mounted in the starboard wing outside the propeller arc.

Fairey's P.27/32, which was powered by a single Rolls-Royce Merlin I engine, had a tare weight of 6,647lb. The tare weight was close to the specification limitation of 6,300lb, but by the time the aircraft had been finalised the limitation was not considered to be of much consequence. The maximum all-up weight was 10,792lb and the maximum wing loading was 25.6lb/sq ft.

The first order for the new Fairey bomber was placed in 1935, for 155 aircraft designated the Battle I. It was the first Merlin I-engined aircraft to be ordered in quantity, and the first production orders for the Rolls-Royce engine were placed in respect of this contract. By March the Battle prototype, K4303, was completed and on the 10th Chris Staniland, Fairey's chief test pilot, took the new bomber into the air for the first time.

Following the preliminary flight test measurements were taken of K4303's performance. During these flights two alternate Merlin I engines, Nos 17 and 25, were installed. No 17 engine gave 958bhp at 12,000ft and No 25 engine 970bhp at the same height.

With engine No 17 cruising speed and range figures were obtained at 14,500ft at a loaded weight of 10,777lb as follows: 904 miles cruising at 220mph, 980 miles at 200mph, 1,030 miles at 180mph, 1,045 miles at an economical speed of 160mph. These figures, with the aircraft carrying a 1,000lb bomb load, were a great advance on any existing type of day bomber in service with Bomber Command.

With engine No 25 a maximum speed of 257mph, with the radiator shutter half open, was recorded. With the shutter full open the maximum speed was 251mph.

At a weight of 10,540lb, and with flaps half open, the Battle prototype stalled at 66mph. Normal landing speed was 53mph, maximum landing run with flaps full down and brakes, was 1,390yd at a weight of 10,540lb. Gliding in at 80mph ASI, K4303 was able to come to rest, from over a 60ft obstacle, in 445yd.

The performance figures obtained were impressive for that time and in most cases were well above the specification requirements. The aircraft was accepted as one of the major types to be produced in very large numbers under the Shadow Factory Scheme.

Following a series of flight trials the first prototype was revised to production standard, which included increased rudder area, a new design of canopy glazing, kidney exhaust pipes and a revised nose incorporating the DH Hamilton variable-pitch propeller in place of the metal fixed-pitch Fairey-Reed unit. This latter item, without a spinner, was less pleasing aesthetically, but was more efficient. In this form, K4303 was shown to the public at the 1936 Hendon RAF Display. A year later the first production Battle I, K7558, made its first flight.

While development of the P.27/32 designs was being actively pursued, the Air Staff issued the requirements for a true Hawker Hart light bomber replacement, under Specification P.4/34. The initial requirements called for a high-performance two-seater day bomber to replace the Hart. Designers were given a free hand as to whether the new aircraft should have one or two engines, as it was thought that some designers might prefer to use two low-powered engines instead of one of high power. The aircraft was to be designed primarily for use in a Continental war and it was to perform the duties of day bombing, dive bombing and strategical reconnaissance. It was also required to act as a fighter bomber, although its design as a fighter should not compromise its function as a fast bomber. As the aircraft had to rely on speed for evasion, high speed was an essential requirement. To this end the speed required was to be the highest obtainable at optimum heights.

The new bomber was required to carry a normal bomb load of 500lb for a range of not less than 600

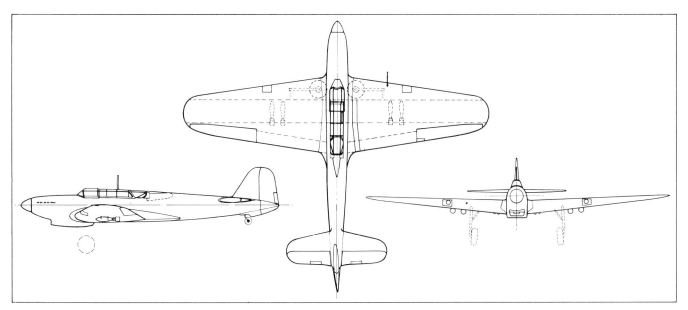

miles at normal cruising engine rpm after half an hour at full throttle. The ceiling was to be not less than 25,000ft and the optimum heights were to be between 10,000 and 20,000ft. The normal bomb load was to consist of 4 x 20lb, 4 x 112lb/120lb bombs, or 2 x 250lb GP bombs. Two additional 250lb bombs were to be carried as overload. The wing span of the new bomber was not to exceed 65ft.

Before the specification was sent out for tender a few changes were made. A single engine was specified, and in addition to the standard range of 600 miles, an auxiliary range of 800 miles was required. Although it was still desired that designers should aim for the highest possible performance, it was thought necessary to stipulate that the top speeds should in any case be not less than 235mph at 5,000ft and 255mph at 15,000ft.

With regard to the bomb load the aircraft was to carry two 250lb AS, SAP or GP bombs. The bomber was also to be able to stow two of the new, larger 250lb Type 'B' anti-heavy warship bombs.

Contracts were placed with the Hawker and Fairey companies for prototypes, two each, of P.4/34 designs.

Hawker's design closely followed the structure that had been evolved for their Hurricane fighter, which itself owed much to earlier biplane design. The outer wings of the P.4/34 were identical in geometry with that of the Hurricane. The fuselage, built around a massive tubular steel warren girder framework, was of clean form. Unlike its Fairey competitor, the Hawker P.4/34 had a deep fuselage, within which was housed the crew of two and a fully-enclosed bomb bay for two 250lb bombs. The aircraft was powered by a single Rolls-Royce Merlin G engine, with the radiator immediately beneath the engine. The radiator intake was in the front of the fuselage. The wing position was low-mid, with the wing spars passing above the bomb bay.

The crew were housed beneath a canopy of unbroken streamlined form, but part of the rear glazing could be opened for the single Lewis gun to be operated. The pilot was provided with a fixed Vickers or Browning gun in the wing. As the outer wings were based on those of the Hurricane, it would have been possible to develop a pure two-seat fighter variant of the bomber, without bomb load, in agreement with the specification requirement.

With a wing span of 47ft 10¼in and an overall length of 36ft, the prototype Hawker P.4/34 was not much larger than the Hurricane and had a top speed of 292mph at 17,100ft. It had a range of 1,000 miles at a cruising speed of 215mph at 15,000ft.

Work on the Hawker P.4/34 progressed slowly, with more man hours being put into development of the Hurricane, but the prototype, K5115, was completed in March 1937 and made its first flight on the 10th of that month. The initial flight and subsequent period of test flying was carried out with K5115 powered by a Merlin F engine, but on June 5, the aircraft was flown with a new engine, a production Merlin I.

Originally designed and built with fabric-covered wings, as on early production Hurricanes, K5115 was given all-metal stressed-skin wings in August, and made its first flight in this form on the 20th. A second prototype, K7554, was completed and flown from Brooklands on May 26, 1938. By this time a production order for 350 aircraft under the type name Henley I had been placed. The metal-winged Henley prototype K5115 weighed 8,393lb fully loaded.

Fairey's P.4/34 design followed the general layout of the Battle day bomber but was smaller, having a wing span of 47ft 4in and an overall length of 40ft. Unlike the Henley the entire airframe was of stressed-skin all-metal construction. A low-wing monoplane, the Fairey P.4/34 carried a crew of two and had an all-up weight of 8,787lb. The bomb load of four 250lb bombs was carried externally under the wings on virtually dragless mountings, for overload missions. The normal load was two 250lb or four 112lb or 120lb bombs.

A clean canopy design covering the two crew members merged with the top line of the fuselage, with a sliding hood for the pilot and a folding windshield for the rear gunner, as on the Battle. The pilot operated a single Vickers or Browning gun in the starboard wing, whereas the rear gunner had a single Lewis gun. As on the Henley, the main undercarriage retracted sideways into the wing, but unlike the Hawker bomber, the tail-wheel was fixed on the Fairey P.4/34.

The Fairey bomber was powered by a single Rolls-Royce Merlin engine, which gave a top speed of 284mph at 17,200ft and 245mph at sea level. It could cruise at 230mph at 15,000ft. Range at 15,000ft was 1,000 miles. Stalling speed was 55mph. Maximum service ceiling was 29,600ft and absolute ceiling 31,000ft.

Two prototypes of the Fairey P.4/34 were ordered, K5099 and K7555. K5099 made its maiden flight on January 13, 1937 and K7555 followed on April 19, 1937. Unlike the Hawker P.4/34, K5115, the basic colour of which was overall Aluminium with polished metal plating, the two Fairey prototypes were painted overall in medium grey. At the time of their early flight trials both prototypes were similar, but later K7555 was fitted with a larger spinner to match the cowling lines.

Although the Fairey design did not receive any orders as a light bomber, the Henley being selected, it in fact eventually fared better, in developed form, as will presently be seen.

The official policy towards the Hart-type of light bomber changed before any of the P.4/34 prototypes

had been completed. It was decided to concentrate on larger, longer-range aircraft, and the order for the Henley was therefore cut to 200 aircraft – all to be adapted for target-towing. They were to prove unsuitable for this role: owing to the drag of the towed targets their Merlin engines had to be run at high power, and consequently engine failures became rife. There was a brief period, during Operation *Banquet*, the anti-invasion preparations in 1940, when it was considered that Henleys might be re-equipped with bomb racks to perform the task for which they were designed, but the idea was dropped when the danger of invasion receded.

The Fairey P.4/34 showed possible development as a fighter during early drafting of the design, and an eight-gun fighter version was eventually adopted by the Danish Government for the use of the Danish Navy. The intention was that it should be built under licence in Denmark and although a production line was duly set up there, the German occupation of Denmark in April 1940 ended the scheme. Meanwhile, the Fleet Air Arm had found itself in urgent need of a two-seat, eight-gun fighter, and early in 1938 the Fairey P.4/34, being readily adaptable for this role, was chosen as the basis of a new design to Specification o.8/38. Thus was born the Fairey Fulmar, which was ordered in quantity and enjoyed a distinguished wartime career.

Below: Hawker P.4/34, Henley I, light bomber. A typical Hawke design, the Henley was similar in structure to the Hind, having fabric covering, over the all-metal internal structure, over much of the airframe. Other parts of the structure were covered by thin metal sheet, highly-polished in the prototypes during the early part of their careers.

Right: The first prototype Hawker Henley, K5115, on test from Brooklands where it was built.

Below right: The second prototype Fairey P.4/34, K7555, and the first prototype Hawker Henley, K5115, seen together at the 1937 RAF Display at Hendon./*The Aeroplane*

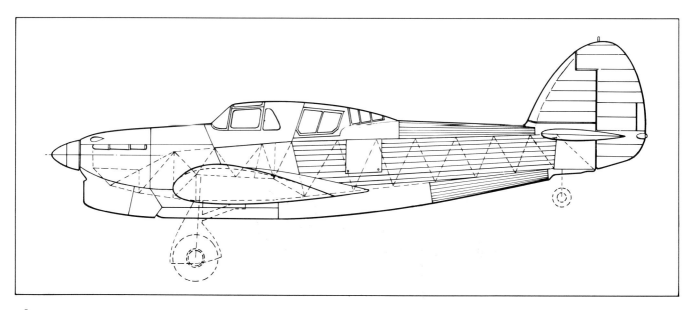

The Heyford and Hendon Replacement Bombers

Birth of the Armstrong Whitworth Whitley (to Specification B.3/34) and Vickers Warwick (to B.1/35).

In 1934 the RAF's heavy night bomber squadrons were flying the Vickers Virginia and Handley Page Heyford twin-engined biplanes. One Auxiliary Air Force Squadron was equipped with the Handley Page Hinaidi, also a twin-engined biplane. The first monoplane night bomber, the Fairey Hendon, was still some two years from entry into service.

At Geneva, the League of Nations Disarmament Conference continued, but with lessening likelihood of agreement. The clause on bomber tare weight limitation, however, still caused the Air Staff to hesitate in formulating new specifications for replacement types to re-equip the night bomber squadrons. In order to evaluate an aircraft which would roughly correspond to the conference tare weight limitation a modified Vickers Vildebeest I general-purpose aircraft (S7715) was tested in the night bomber role at the RAE, Farnborough, by No 7 (Virginia bomber) Squadron and at the A & AEE, Martlesham Heath. It was thought that this aircraft could be adapted as an interim night bomber, carrying a maximum bomb load of 1,500lb at 140mph at 6,500ft, but its range of 660 miles with this load was considered insufficient. At this time it was held that a satisfactory night bomber would have to have a range of 920 miles when carrying a 1,500lb bomb load, and be able to land at night at 55mph.

Early in 1934 the tare weight restriction had not yet been abandoned, and a possible solution to the need to develop a new night bomber was to modify the B.9/32 designs to carry a bigger bomb load over a longer range, and yet land at slower speed. This would mean designing wings of greater area, with possibly bigger tail units, as well. The suggestion was made that these designs should have wings that could be quickly changed if the aircraft were to carry out night bombing attacks, but this could also possibly mean designing changeable tail units. Such a scheme seemed im-

Vickers Vildebeest I S7715 and Vickers Valentia K3603 fly in formation. The Vildebeest was evaluated by the Air Ministry as a makeshift night bomber complete with the standard dark green Nivo night bomber finish.

practical. On June 7, 1934, the tare weight limitation was officially abandoned and this made it possible to issue a revised set of requirements for the night bomber replacement. It was realised that much valuable time had been lost in trying to develop a lightweight design to a requirement that was always associated with very big heavy aeroplanes.

The Chief of the Air Staff was concerned about the lack of progress on the Hendon and Heyford replacement and suggested that a selected company should be given a free hand to design the best night bomber of which it was capable. It was also suggested that a big bomber should be ordered from America in order to learn as much as possible about their latest technology.

A revised specification, B.3/34, was drawn up. This called for a heavy bomber landplane (the title 'night bomber' was now changed to 'heavy bomber' because it was considered that the aircraft could also operate by day in heavy cloud cover) with a wing span not exceeding 100ft. It was to have a crew of five, two pilots, two air gunners, and a W/T operator. One pilot was to act as navigator, and the W/T operator could also man a third gun position. The aircraft was to carry a 2,500lb bomb load over a range of 1,250 miles at 15,000ft. Maximum speeds were to be 205mph at 5,000ft and 225mph at 15,000ft. The bomb load could consist of 8 x 20lb bombs, 16 x 112lb bombs, 16 x 120lb bombs, 10 x 250lb bombs, 4 x 500lb bombs, 2 x 1,000lb bombs, or 1 x 1,500lb bomb. Maximum ferry range with auxiliary tanks was to be 1,000 miles.

The specification draft was sent to Vickers, Fairey, Handley Page and Armstrong Whitworth on July 23, 1934, and representatives from these companies and the Air Ministry were invited to a conference on the B.3/34 on August 1, 1934. At this time it was agreed to reduce the maximum speed of the aircraft to 205mph, provided that a tail turret was fitted, and to decrease the rate of climb, allowing 20 minutes for the climb to 15,000ft. The requirement to carry the 1,000lb and 1,500lb bombs was deleted.

The conference on August 1 proved to be unsuccessful, with all the company representatives failing to agree to a price for producing a prototype B.3/34. The companies wanted at least £60,000 for development costs on the new bomber, pointing out that the Martin XB-10 prototype had cost £100,000 to develop. The conference broke up without any decision.

After the failure of the conference the Air Staff considered that it would be better to select one contractor for the B.3/34 and offer a fixed price of £32,000 for each prototype, and the reward of a substantial production contract if the bomber met the requirements. Two companies were selected, Vickers and Armstrong Whitworth. Vickers' B.3/34 design was based on their B.9/32 bomber, utilising the same basic fuselage structure with larger wings and tail unit. As the Vickers design was of Wallis' geodetic structure, as yet untried, it was thought to be unwise to order another

geodetic aircraft in addition to the G.4/31 and B.9/32 aircraft. Thus the choice of the contractor was Armstrong Whitworth and the B.3/34 development contract was placed with this Coventry-based firm.

The Air Staff suggested that if Vickers wanted to develop their B.3/34 as a private venture design the Air Ministry would be prepared to lend two engines to the company without charge, and would be prepared to pay £40,000 for a prototype. But a production contract would not be guaranteed. Vickers did not take up this offer.

Armstrong Whitworth's B.3/34 was based on experience with their C.26/31 bomber-transport design, the AW23, although in construction it greatly differed, particularly in fuselage design. The fuselage of the AW23 was constructed of tubular steel with fabric covering, whereas that of the B.3/34 bomber was an all-metal stressed skin monocoque.

The new bomber was given the Armstrong Whitworth design number 38, and it was powered initially by two Armstrong Siddeley Tiger 14-cylinder air-cooled radial engines of 795hp each. The AW38, unlike the AW23, was a mid-wing monoplane with the wing set at a high angle of incidence. Although this unusual wing design feature created higher drag than with a wing of less incidence because of the nose-down angle of the fuselage when the wing was in cruising or high speed flight attitude, it bestowed a lower landing speed for night operations. In later years the nose-down angle at which the Armstrong Whitworth bomber flew became a familiar and instantly recognisable hallmark which assisted those concerned with aircraft recognition.

The tail unit consisted of twin fins and rudders mounted on a low set tailplane, the fins being strut-braced to the fuselage. The tail unit was a metal structure covered in fabric. The thick wing was built around a massive all-metal box spar which was the main load-carrying structural member. This spar extended to the upper and lower contours of the wing. Attached to the forward face of the spar was an all-metal leading edge, metal skinned, which contained fuel and oil tanks. The light metal structure, aft of the box spar was fabric covered and the inner section contained cells for lighter types of bombs. The main bomb load was housed in two fuselage bays either side of the box spar/fuselage intersection structure. Small bombs were stowed in a separate small bay aft of the lower turret.

In the extreme nose was a single Lewis gun on a moveable mounting, covered by a Perspex cupola. The bomb aimer's position, beneath the front turret, was provided with an opening window similar to that used

Above Right: The Armstrong Whitworth AW23 bomber-cum-troop carrier, built to Specification C.26/31, and (*right*) the first prototype AW 38 Whitley bomber whose design it greatly influenced.

on earlier heavy bombers, but in later variants of the bomber the draughty, open window was replaced by an enclosed sighting window. The tail gunner was provided with a single Lewis gun on a moveable mounting, with a similar turret to that installed in the front position. A retractable "dustbin" turret, housing twin machine guns, was mounted in the fuselage underside immediately below the wing trailing edge. Wing span of the AW38 was 84ft, the overall length 69ft 3in and the overall height 15ft. The wing area was 1,137sq ft.

Work on the AW38 progressed well, and in August 1935 an initial production order for 80 aircraft was placed, which allowed Armstrong Whitworth to proceed with the setting up of a production line to speed up delivery of the type to squadrons. By now the name Whitley I had officially been given to the new heavy bomber. By March 1936 the first prototype Whitley was complete and on the 17th of that month A. C. Campbell-Orde took the new bomber into the air from the company's airfield at Baginton, near Coventry.

Test flying of this prototype, K4586, soon established that the design was very satisfactory and that major modifications to the initial production versions would not be necessary. An assessment of the Whitley's speed performance was carried out when powered by the Tiger IX engines of 795hp each. At 7,000ft the Whitley reached a speed of 192mph. 180mph was attained at 3,000ft, and 189.5mph at 13,000ft. At 16,500ft 183.5mph was reached. Cruising at 66 per cent power the Whitley reached 160mph compared with 120mph for the Hendon, 115mph for the Heyford and about 70mph for the Virginia – clearly a substantial advance. Range with normal bomb load was 1,250 miles and maximum ferry range was 1,600 miles. Empty weight of the Whitley I was 14,272lb and normal loaded weight 21,660lb.

A second Whitley I prototype, K4587, joined the test programme during 1936, followed by the first production aircraft in March 1937. Further versions were under development and these are detailed in chapter 5.

When the original B.3/34 specification was issued, it was known as Specification No 1 – the new bomber was required to also act if necessary as a troop carrier. After the failure of the conference on August 1, 1934, and the subsequent ordering of the B.3/34 from Armstrong Whitworth, the troop carrying requirement was dropped from the specification and the original maximum speed of 225mph was reduced to 205mph. In this form the Specification B.3/34, to which the Whitley was designed, was known as Specification No 2. (It is interesting to note that troop carrying eventually became one of the Whitley's wartime roles).

While the B.3/34 decision was being implemented with the aircraft being ordered from the Coventry firm, the Director of Technical Development was sent to America to tour American companies to obtain in-

formation on what designers there were developing in the bomber field. It had originally been intended to issue the No 2 specification to open tender to other companies, in case the Armstrong Whitworth bomber proved to have shortcomings, but this was held over until the return of the team from America. It was considered that the specification would be revised to order a superior type to the original B.3/34 specifications. This Americanised specification was known as Specification No 3.

In the light of bomber design trends in America, Specification No 3 was revised in a number of ways. The maximum speed of the aircraft was raised to 230mph and the new requirement for load carrying was that it should be able to carry 2,000lb of bombs for a range of 2,000 miles cruising at 150mph. With range reduced to 1,500 miles the bomb load was to be capable of being increased to 3,000lb. A bomb load of 4,000lb was to be carried for 1,000 miles. The new bomber was to have three defensive gunners' positions, one in the nose and two aft of the mainplane. The revised bomb load was to incorporate the carriage of either sixteen 250lb or eight 500lb bombs. There were a number of other detail changes from the Nos 1 and 2 specifications.

The new requirements outlined in Specification No 3 would be expected to result in a much larger aeroplane than that resulting from the two earlier B.3/34 specifications, and this caused some discussion before the new specification was issued to the aircraft industry for tender.

Head-on view of the first prototype Whitley, K4586, showing the absence of dihedral on the upper surface of the wing – a feature common to the second prototype and, in its initial form the Whitley I.

Some years earlier two bomber-transport prototypes, the Gloster TC33 and Vickers Type 163, had been built to Specification C.16/28. Both were very large four-engined biplanes, and although both had been successful as flying machines and met the specification requirements, their sheer size and bulk had made them difficult to handle, particularly on the ground. Their wing spans made them unacceptable in existing hangars and their weight made ground handling a major problem. For this reason the C.16/28 specification had been abandoned and it had been necessary to order new bomber-transports to a revised lighter specification, the C.26/31, which resulted in such prototypes as the Bristol Bombay, Handley Page HP43 and HP51 and AW23.

Experience with the C.16/28 prototypes made the Air Ministry limit the wing span of new heavy aircraft to 100ft, and if possible to restrict the all-up weight to about 20,000lb, although the weight limit eventually proved to be impracticable. The 100ft wing span limit became a standard feature of all new specifications for large aeroplanes for land-based use, and this tended to limit the all-up weight of large bombers if the wing loading was to be kept within the accepted limits for the period.

By the time the B.3/34 Specification No 3 was ready to be sent out to tender it was March 1935. The specification was issued under the new designation B.1/35 and a letter stating requirements for the new bomber was sent to most of the companies of the industry on March 25. The new bomber was regarded as a potential B.3/34 replacement. From the designs

tendered three were selected for prototype development and possible production, the Handley Page, Armstrong Whitworth and Vickers designs. Contracts for the development of these prototypes were placed with the companies in September 1935.

The Armstrong Whitworth B.1/35 was initially to be powered by two Rolls-Royce Merlins, and the other two firms' design projects by Bristol Hercules engines. The Armstrong Whitworth B.1/35 was closely allied to the Whitley, using some of the earlier aircraft's components. Unlike the Whitley the fuselage had a stepped top line, with nose, mid-upper and tail turrets. The two Merlin engines were installed in short nacelles. Another engine installation, using the Armstrong Siddeley Deerhound 21-cylinder, three-row air-cooled radial engine in faired nacelles, was projected. In this case the engine was almost entirely buried in the wing leading edge. Air testing of the Deerhound (albeit not as a buried installation) was eventually done in a standard Whitley II, K7243, which first flew with two of the new engines in January 1939 and continued in this experimental role until destroyed in a fatal crash in March 1940.

Vickers' B.1/35 project, in its original form, was basically an enlarged version of the Vickers B.9/32,

By now, the second prototype, L9704, was nearing completion and it was hoped that the increased engine power provided by its two Bristol Centaurus CE1SM engines would restore the aircraft's performance. L9704 was flown for the first time on April 5, 1940, by 'Mutt' Summers, and it was at once obvious that it was a big improvement over K8178. It had been the intention to install Napier Sabre engines in K8178, but priority for this engine was given to the Hawker Typhoon. Although successful in the Vickers B.1/35, the Centaurus engine was not yet available in sufficient quantities for it to be considered the initial production engine; a further problem was that the Vulture was proving to be far from satisfactory and seemed unlikely to continue long in production. Accordingly, in July 1940 the suggestion of fitting American Pratt & Whitney engines was made, and it was decided to install and test fly Double Wasps in L9704.

In January 1941 a production order was placed for 250 Double Wasp-powered Vickers B.1/35s under the type name Warwick B.I. Directional stability continued to be unsatisfactory on the prototypes, and at one stage it was proposed to fit twin fins and rudders. Development work on the tail unit eventually improved the control problems, but the Warwick never entered service in the bomber role for which it had been designed; thus the B.1/35 specification did not succeed in producing a Whitley (B.3/34) replacement as had been intended. Instead, development of the P.13/36 designs, the Halifax and Manchester (and, of course,

Above: The first prototype Vickers B.1/35 Warwick K8178, as completed with Rolls-Royce Vulture engines.

Above right: The second prototype Warwick, L9704, powered by two Bristol Centaurus CEISM engines, photographed in April 1940, the month in which it first flew.

Right: By the time the first production Warwick B.I, BV214, seen here, appeared (April 1942) the requirement for the Warwick bomber no longer existed. However, the design, after further development, did eventually see service in the transport, air sea rescue and maritime reconnaissance roles.

the latter's subsequent development, the Lancaster) ensured that Bomber Command had new aircraft to follow the Whitley in the heavy, long-range night bomber role.

It is probable that had the Vickers B.1/35 been constructed of any orthodox structural system it would have been cancelled earlier in its career, but there was much interest in geodetic structures, and the need to keep development of this structural method certainly influenced some of the decisions taken at official levels. Although the aircraft was never intended to be the Wellington successor, as had been frequently stated by some sources, it was considered, late in its development, that it could be used for this purpose – mainly because the B.I had a similar overall performance to the Wellington B.III but carried a much heavier bomb load. The Halifax, Stirling and Manchester could, however, carry heavier bomb loads at higher speed, and the Warwick was found other roles.

**Second Generation
Heavy Bombers
to B.12/36**

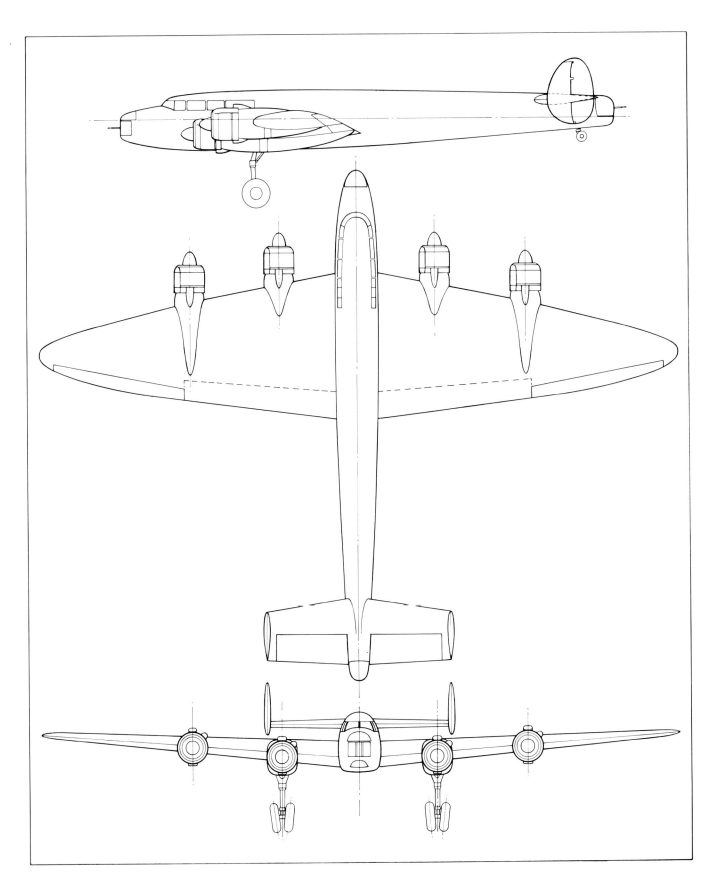

Above: The Vickers-Armstrongs Supermarine B.12/36 four-engined heavy bomber, powered by Bristol Hercules engines. This was the last aircraft design on which R. J. Mitchell worked. Two prototypes were ordered, L6889 and L6890. Both were destroyed by bombing when partially built.

Right: An impression of the Vickers-Armstrongs Supermarine B.12/36 as it would have appeared in 1940.

than a lightly-equipped aerodynamic shell, albeit of great potential. It was Joe Smith who was to guide its development into a potent fighting aircraft and was eventually to add 100mph to its top speed by progressive development.

The original draft of the Supermarine bomber adopted a wing planform with a straight trailing edge and sweepback from the root to the tip on the leading edge alone. The tail unit had a single fin and rudder. This design evolved into the finalised form, which adopted a wing planform with more equal taper, but with more on the leading than trailing edge, and with twin fins and rudders.

Supermarine's four-engined bomber was projected with several alternative engine installations. The primary version was powered by Bristol Hercules HE1SM sleeve-valve radial engines, with Rolls-Royce Merlin in-line engines as a second choice. Napier Dagger engines were also considered.

The Type 316 featured a single-spar wing constructed with hollow tapered extrusions for the spar booms. The wing section forward of the spar formed the integral fuel tanks, but as these were part of the wing structure it is not known what method was to be provided to make them meet the later requirement to have self-sealing properties. The monospar wing layout was adopted to provide stowage space for a major part of the bomb load behind the spar. This was carried well out across the wing span, in 10 bomb cells extending

out beyond the outer nacelle in each wing to relieve bending loads on the wing in flight, and reduce the size of the fuselage by discarding the need for a large fuselage bomb bay. Twenty 250lb bombs could be stowed in the wing cells, with nine more in the short fuselage bay. Four 2,000lb AP bombs could be carried in the cells between the fuselage and inner engine nacelles, with three more in the fuselage bay. 500lb bombs could be carried in the wing and fuselage bays, and the maximum weight of bombs carried was 13,500lb.

During the later war years the emphasis changed to the carriage of smaller numbers of very heavy bombs with high blast effect for the destruction of area targets. The general policy behind the B.12/36 designs was to carry as many bombs as possible in a single aeroplane, so that if the number of bombers was limited a target could be saturated with 250lb or 500lb bombs. Future raids by, say, 600 four-engined bombers using bombs of 4,000lb, 8,000lb and 12,000lb weight, as carried out in the later war years, could not have been anticipated in 1936 and 1937. It is difficult to assess how the Supermarine bomber would have fared in the light of the changing strategy, but its multiple wing cells housing the major part of the bomb load would have become largely redundant, its fuselage bay was too small to house large bombs, and its wing structure, without the relief of weight out along the span afforded by the wing bomb loading, would not have been

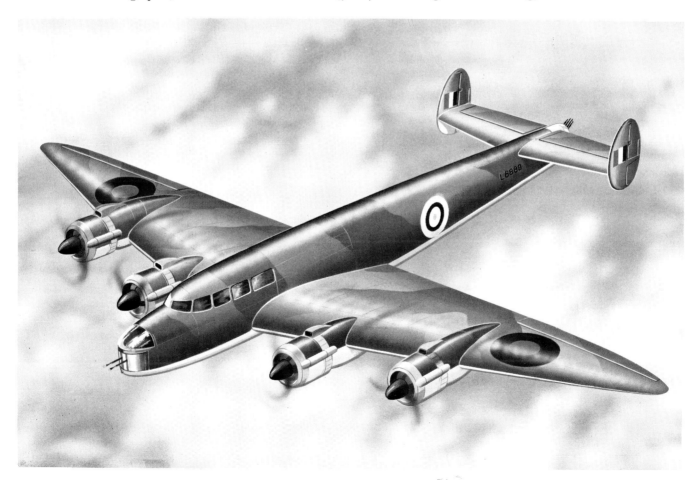

stressed to carry heavy central loads in the fuselage even if this had been physically possible.

The Supermarine Type 316 was designed to mount Vickers-Armstrongs power-operated turrets. Twin .303in machine guns were to be installed in the front turret, two more in a ventral retractable turret, and a further four in the rear turret. It is probable that had the Type 316 been put into production the front and rear turrets would have been changed to Frazer-Nash designs mounting similar numbers of weapons. It is also probable that the ventral turret would have been replaced by a mid-upper turret.

Twin-wheel designs were used for the main and tail undercarriage units, all of which were retractable.

Original estimates of performance gave a top speed of 329mph when powered by four Bristol Hercules HE1SM engines. At a weight of 58,380lb it was estimated that it would cruise at 279mph, carrying an 8,000lb bomb load. The landing speed was expected to be 84mph.

As design development advanced the weight of the Type 316 inevitably increased and a more detailed and accurate assessment of its performance could be made. Its tare weight was expected to be 29,500lb, considerably lighter than that of the Short B.12/36. At a lightly loaded weight of 44,790lb, the Type 316 could carry 2,000lb of bombs for 1,500 miles at 273mph. It was estimated that 4,000lb of bombs could be carried for 2,000 miles at a weight of 50,200lb, cruising at 270mph.

At an all-up weight of 60,500lb a maximum range of 3,000 miles could be attained, carrying an 8,000lb bomb load and cruising at 265mph. At 59,900lb, if the range was reduced to 2,000 miles, it was estimated that a maximum bomb of 13,500lb could be carried – again cruising at 265mph.

With weight reduced to 58,000lb, an 11,500lb bomb load could be carried at 266mph for 2,000 miles. Maximum level speed was expected to be 317mph.

It is possible, in view of the history of many projects, that in practice these performance figures would have been slightly reduced – depending, of course, on engine performance. The Supermarine bomber was, however, smaller and lighter than its Short Brothers counterpart, and its performance on similar engines should therefore have been generally higher. Performance figures for the Merlin-powered version are not available, but would have been similar to those attainable with the Hercules-powered Type 316.

Design work on the new bomber had, by early autumn of 1937, reached a stage when a wooden mock-up of the new aircraft could be constructed to assist in positioning of equipment, cable and pipe runs, etc, and to assess various aspects of the real aeroplane, such as crew comfort and vision for pilots and gunners. This was completed and inspected by representatives of the Air Staff and Air Ministry on October 5, 1937. A design conference on the Supermarine B.12/36 was held on December 20 between representatives of the Air Staff and Air Ministry, and Vickers-Armstrongs, including Joe Smith and Rex Pierson.

By this time half of the working drawings for construction of the prototypes had been issued to the Experimental Department workshops. Work at this stage progressed rapidly, but the success of the Spitfire and their other commitments on production of flying boats caused Supermarine to become overloaded with work. Supermarine was a comparatively small company in 1936, producing limited numbers of flying boats, but by 1937 the Spitfire had shown such potential that orders for 510 Mk Is had been received. The company also had substantial orders for Stranraers and Walruses. The Spitfire orders were massive by any standards, and all available effort had to be put into organising the works to ensure that these contracts could be met. Development and construction of the B.12/36 therefore had to take second place and slowed down in consequence.

It may be that the Air Ministry was unwise to select the Supermarine design for prototype development in view of that company's size and possible future production commitments, but in 1936 the Spitfire's potential had yet to be realised. All other companies in the aircraft industry were heavily engaged on design or production of new aircraft for the RAF, and Supermarine had, by some standards, a comparatively light work load. The immediate success of the Spitfire changed the situation, and by the end of 1936 310 Mk Is were on order, with a second order for a further 200 following in 1937.

Construction of two prototypes of the Supermarine B.12/36 continued on a low key basis in the Woolston works of Supermarine at Southampton. Work on the two Supermarine prototypes, L6889 and L6890 continued slowly during the first year of the war with the main emphasis on Spitfire production and development. The Battle of Britain was at its height and production of fighters was given priority over all other types. On September 26, in the late afternoon, 59 Heinkel He 111s of KG.55 laid an accurately-delivered 'bomb carpet' across the Woolston factory, and in the wrecked works the partially-constructed prototypes were damaged beyond repair.

The destruction of the prototypes dealt a mortal blow to the Supermarine B.12/36 programme, although it is not certain that these aircraft would ever have been completed. At the time of their destruction the prototypes were at least a year behind schedule and Supermarine was already stretched to the limit on Spitfire production. It may be that had the prototypes progressed more quickly and had been flown early in 1939 the fate of the design would have been different. Had the aircraft proved to be outstanding during flight trials, as seemed possible from the design assessment, the history of British heavy bomber development may have taken a different course. Had the two

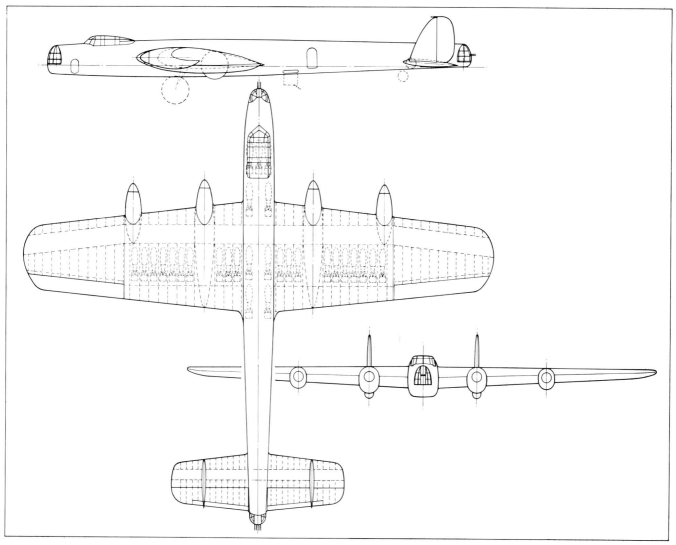

B.12/36 designs, the Stirling and Supermarine Type 316, both gone into production and proved to be successful, with the Halifax as a third four-engined bomber, it is probable that the Lancaster would not have been evolved – to the detriment of Bomber Command. Had the Type 316 proved to be a successful aircraft in squadron service it is also possible that the Halifax may have been discontinued when it ran into serious, if temporary, problems – instead of being modified and developed into the potent bomber that it was to become.

On balance, however, it seems more likely that the very specialised design of the integral wing tankage, with its vulnerability and the problems of providing self-sealing properties, the distribution of the main bomb load in individual cells far out across the wing, and the small fuselage bomb bay, would have brought about the early demise of the Supermarine B.12/36. Had it flown, it would probably have proved to be faster than the Stirling and would have had a better altitude performance, but it would have been subject to the same bomb size limitations and its usefulness would have been restricted. This was common to all B.12/36 designs, and it was this latter requirement that

The Armstrong Whitworth B.12/36 heavy bomber, powered by four Rolls-Royce Merlin engines. It is not known what radiator system was intended to be installed from the original company drawing, but is likely that each engine would have had a 'chin' radiator. The drawing shows the distribution of the load of 250lb bombs. This aircraft was not ordered. Span was 100ft and length was 90ft.

was to give the advantage to all those designs based on the P.13/36 Specification.

Unlike the B.12/36, the P.13/36 had, beside the carriage of large numbers of 250lb and 500lb bombs, to carry two 18in torpedoes in the fuselage bay – which, because of their bulk, necessitated the bomb bay being unrestricted by individual bomb cells. This feature, in the Halifax and Manchester (and, of course, the Lancaster) permitted much bigger bombs to be carried in later years. It is ironic that torpedoes were never, in fact, carried operationally by the P.13/36 designs or their developments.

Other unsuccessful tenders for the B.12/36 orders were designed by Bristol, de Havilland, Vickers-Armstrongs and Armstrong Whitworth.

Plans for a New Medium Bomber

Birth of the Avro Manchester and Handley Page Halifax.

Concurrent with plans for the development of a long-range four-engined bomber the Air Staff were formulating requirements for a new tactical medium bomber capable of being operated in any part of the world. The bomber was to be a harder-hitting replacement for such types as the Wellington and Hampden, and it was to be capable of flexible loadings giving variations of bomb load and range according to operational requirements. It therefore had to have provision for a heavy bomb load and extensive fuel tankage.

A system of catapult launching from land aerodromes was under active development by the Royal Aircraft Establishment at Farnborough, with the intention of launching heavy bombers with both maximum bomb and fuel loads. This would permit a bomber to carry a very heavy bomb load over ranges unattainable from normal take-off methods from then-standard size airfields. Tests were being conducted at Farnborough, catapulting a Virginia IX, with promising results. Such a take-off method applied to the then-new production bombers such as the Whitley, Wellington and Hampden would have raised problems of re-stressing these airframes for catapult loads, but it could easily be added as a requirement in a new specification.

The new bomber requirement was outlined· in the issue of Specification P.13/36 (specifications for tactical aircraft were given the prefix 'P'), and a meeting was held on June 22, 1936, at the Air Ministry at which the Operational Requirements Committee discussed

plans for the new bomber. The original speed requirement of 220mph was questioned, as it might not be sufficient in, say, four years hence. It was therefore increased in the specification. There was discussion whether the P.13/36 should have four engines for safety, but it was decided to use two large engines. It was considered that the type might be used as a torpedo-bomber, with four torpedoes installed, but this requirement was reduced to two. Besides the normal turret armament it was considered that beam mounted Vickers 'K' guns should be installed. It was also considered that the front turret might be eliminated, but this was overruled. The specification was now ready for issue.

Specification P.13/36 called for a twin-engined medium bomber capable of being used throughout the world and having the highest possible cruising speed to reduce time spent over enemy territory. Defence was to be provided by at least nose and tail turrets, power-operated. The aircraft was to cruise at 275mph at two-thirds maximum engine power at maximum cruising rpm at normal loading. (This figure for cruising speed was to prove unattainable at normal loaded weight with any of the designs directly resulting from the P.13/36 specification).

At normal loading, with a take-off of 500 yards, the bomber was required to carry 1,000lb of bombs for 1,000 miles minimum range at 15,000ft altitude whilst cruising at maximum cruising engine rpm. In both of these cases these performance figures were to be obtained after spending $\frac{1}{4}$hr at maximum sea level power.

Using catapult take-off technique the bomber was to be able to carry not less than 4,000lb of bombs for at least 3,000 miles under the same power ratings as the previous cases. Under catapult take-off conditions a maximum bomb load of at least 8,000lb was to be carried for 2,000 miles. Maximum range for the

The first prototype Avro 679 Manchester, L7246, in August 1939 shortly after its maiden flight and before the addition of gun turrets and a central fin.

P.13/36 was to be 3,000 miles. The service ceiling (maximum altitude) at normal loaded weight was to be at least 28,000ft, with 10,000ft attainable at normal weight with one engine stopped and the aircraft in level flight.

In the P.13/36 specification provision was requested for a crew of four – two pilots, wireless operator and one air gunner. It is interesting to note that the duties of bomb aimer, navigator and front gunner were all to be performed by one of the two pilots – reflecting an attempt to economise on air crew personnel by putting an excessive work load on the pilots. In practice this was found to be unworkable and the crews of such bombers were increased to six or seven.

The specification requirement regarding crew members was based on those operating the new production bombers, the Whitley and Wellington, in which the second pilot did perform the additional duties of front gunner, navigator and bomb aimer until changed through experience. The crews of the Whitley and Wellington were increased to five and even this number proved to be insufficient to operate the big aeroplanes developed to Specifications B.12/36 and P.13/36. In Specification P.13/36 and presumably also in B.12/36, provision had to be made to accommodate a relief pilot or navigator, as well as a relief observer/wireless operator or air gunner to help operate the aircraft on long-distance flights.

Provision was to be made to install a twin .303 gun turret in the nose, with a four .303in gun turret at the rear. Each gun had to have at least 1,000 rounds of ammunition, with 1,500 rounds if possible for the aft guns. A reserve of 6,000 rounds was to be carried, although this could be reduced to 4,000 rounds if the rear guns had normal provision for 1,500 rounds each. A maximum bomb load of 8,000lb was to be carried in the following loads: 16 x 500lb bombs; 16 x 250lb bombs or 4 x 2,000 AP bombs. Provision was also to be made to carry two 18in torpedoes.

The P.13/36 aeroplanes were to be designed to carry out the functions of general reconnaissance and general purpose in addition to the primary role of tactical medium bomber. (Of the types developed from P.13/36 only the Handley Page Halifax was used for roles other than bombing during World War II – performing the additional roles of maritime general reconnaissance, glider-towing, and army support).

The new specification was sent to a number of companies in the aircraft industry and tenders were invited. Two designs from those submitted were to be selected for prototype development and probable production. Because of the requirement to carry a heavy bomb load over long range and to have the capacity to vary the bomb load/range loading (ie to select maximum range with a small bomb load, maximum bomb load, for a short range, or various combinations of bomb load and range, as required by the operational needs at a particular moment), the P.13/36 bomber was expected to

be big for a twin-engined aeroplane. It was therefore likely to require engines of around 2,000hp each. Fortunately designers had the choice of at least three engines in this class which were under active development at that time. These were the Rolls-Royce Vulture, Napier Sabre and Bristol Centaurus, of which the Vulture was by far the most advanced in its development programme. This big engine used an 'X' layout for its 24 cylinders, being virtually two Peregrine engines, one in normal attitude and one inverted, on a common crankshaft. This gave a power rating of 1,750hp, with promise of more to come with development.

The Sabre engine was an entirely new and advanced-technology design, of 'H' configuration for its 24 cylinders and expected to attain well over 2,000hp. It was, however, only at the early stage of its development.

The Bristol Centaurus, again at an early stage of development, was an 18 cylinder, air-cooled, sleeve valve, radial engine of twin-row design. It, too, was expected to be rated well over 2,000hp. Because of its stage of development the Vulture engine was selected by most designers as the primary engine installation for their P.13/36 projects. At this stage it was an engine of great promise and its later problems could not be foreseen.

One of the project designs submitted that gained favour was produced by Avro under the company's Type number 679. The Avro 679 represented an enormous step into the unknown for its designers. It was one of the biggest and heaviest aeroplanes ever projected by Avro, had the highest wing loading, and incorporated a stressed skin, all-metal structure. To these unknowns was added the problems associated with the installation of a new and untried engine of much higher power than any previously used.

In spite of some early setbacks, so successfully did the Avro team overcome the design problems, and such was the structural and aerodynamic design integrity, that the new bomber was the sire to a long succession of direct descendants covering a period of some 30 years – the Lancaster, York, Lincoln, Shackleton and Argosy, with their derivatives, all of which have aerodynamic or structural features common to the family line.

The Avro 679 was an all-metal, mid-wing monoplane of 80ft 2in span, with an overall length of 69ft 4½in. It was powered by two Rolls-Royce Vulture engines of 1,750hp each. The new bomber was designed to have power-operated gun turrets in the extreme nose and tail, with a third, retractable, turret in the belly position. The nose and ventral turrets housed twin .303in Browning guns, whilst the rear turret had four of these weapons installed.

Originally the tail unit was designed with inset twin fins and rudders, but the eventual design incorporated small end-plate fins mounted on the low-set tailplane. The pilots and navigator's compartments were covered by a large canopy. In the initial layout of the big bomber this was of streamlined form fairing down into the upper fuselage, but in the finalised design this canopy terminated at the astrodome. This gave excellent pilot vision.

An important feature of the Avro 679 was the immense bomb bay – designed to amply meet the requirement to carry two 18in torpedoes (as well as a big load of 250lb or 500lb bombs) in the torpedo-bomber role. This large volume, unobstructed bomb bay, some 34ft long, was to prove invaluable in later years in the Avro 679 and its famous successor, the Lancaster, in accommodating bombs of larger bulk and length than any imagined in pre-war days. Fore and aft stress loads were carried through the massive bomb bay roof structure, which again proved its worth in later years in being able to support very heavy bombs.

Like the other P.13/36 designs, the Avro 679 was stressed for catapult launching and dive bombing. Although catapult launching was never used operationally and dive bombing was carried out only in a shallow dive on rare occasions, these attributes had a secondary benefit in ensuring that the P.13/36 designs were strong enough to stand up to violent evasive action. Catapult launching of one of the Avro 679 prototypes was carried out at Farnborough, but the acceptance of the use of bigger airfields, higher take-off speeds and longer take-off runs made this complicated method of launching a heavily loaded bomber unnecessary. The provision at airfields of the catapult mechanism would have been costly, and the continual re-loading of heavily-laden bombers into the mechanism would have made the despatch of a number of aircraft on a sortie a slow and laborious business.

The new Avro bomber was accepted for prototype development under the type name Manchester I and the serial numbers L7246 and L7247 were allotted to the two prototypes. Plans for possible future production

The Avro Type 679, P.13/36, twin-engined bomber. This was the prototype for the Manchester and is shown in its original form, without turrets, and with small fins. The wing span of this prototype, L7246, was 80ft 2in and the length was 69ft 4½in. The span of production-type Manchesters was 90ft 1in.

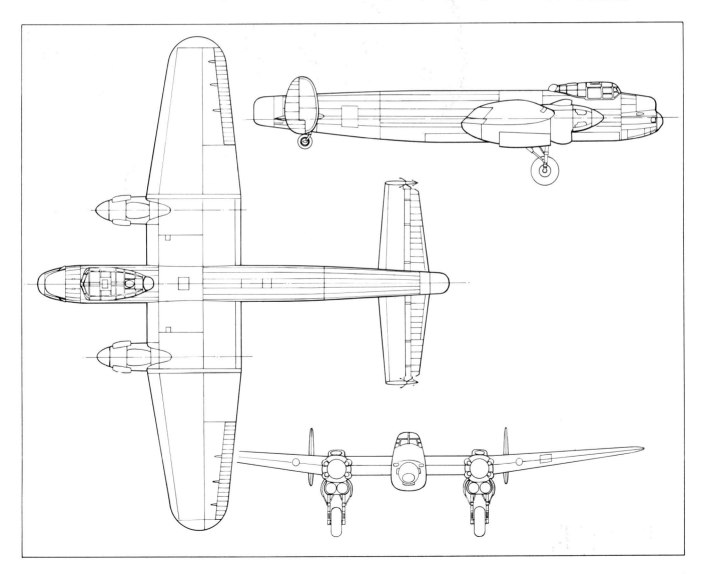

were drawn up and in 1937 two hundred Manchesters were ordered.

By the early summer of 1939, L7246, the first Manchester, was completed and prepared for initial flight trials. At this stage this prototype did not have the power-operated turrets fitted, the positions being faired over. The prototype was finished in Dark Green/Dark Earth/Night camouflage, with Type A.1 roundels and large white under-wing serials.

On July 25, 1939, the new bomber was flown for the first time by Capt H. A. Brown, from Ringway, Manchester. Unlike the majority of new and important events in aviation at that time the trials were conducted in secrecy and mention of the aircraft by name was not made for about a year after the first flight, and photographs were not made available for publication until much later.

The early flight trials of the Manchester prototype were not successful. The Vulture engines were not giving full take-off power, and this, combined with the high wing loading of the aircraft, made the new bomber unsatisfactory to handle in the air. It was also obvious from these early flight tests that the Manchester was unstable directionally, due to the insufficient area of the two small fins and rudders. A third, centrally-mounted, fin was added, as the easiest solution to the directional problem. After several different fin configurations had been test flown a satisfactory shape was evolved for possible future production.

In spite of these early set-backs and difficulties the Manchester showed great promise and development potential for the future, although persistent troubles with the Vulture engine continued to give rise to concern over the future of the big Rolls-Royce engine. At the time of the first flight the future importance of the Avro P.13/36 design as the sire of Bomber Command's most outstanding heavy bomber was not foreseen, but other engines were being considered for the Manchester as an insurance against the failure of the Vulture.

Meanwhile, production of the Manchester had commenced at Avro's Manchester factories, and a second main production line started in 1939 at Metropolitan Vickers' factory at Trafford Park (Manchester) – with final assembly in both cases at Avro's Woodford factory.

L7247, the second Manchester prototype, was flown for the first time on May 26, 1940. This aircraft had the gun turrets fitted, and had the three-fin tail configuration. At a later date almost 10 feet was added to the wing span to lessen the wing loading and improve the bomber's take-off characteristics.

Production of the Manchester gained momentum during early 1940 and by the end of July the first production aircraft, L7276, was complete and ready for flight trials. The first Manchester squadron, No 207, was formed in November 1940, but it was not operational until 1941.

Another tender for the P.13/36 contract was sub-mitted by Hawker. This mid-wing design was similar to the Avro bomber in general layout and similarly-powered by Rolls-Royce Vultures. It had a wing span of 87ft and an overall length of 72ft 8in. Tailplane span was 32ft. It had a wing area of 1,080sq ft and a total fuel capacity of 1,820 gallons. The main bomb or torpedo load was carried in the large volume fuselage bomb bay, but there were six wing bomb cells in the centre portion of the wing, between the nacelles and fuselage. A twin .303in gun turret was installed in the front, with a four-gun rear turret.

The Hawker P.13/36 was not accepted for prototype development, probably largely due to the heavy work load with which Hawker was confronted – which included production and development of the Hurricane and development of the Henley, Tornado and Typhoon. Another factor against the Hawker design may have been the company's inexperience in the design and construction of very big aeroplanes.

Handley Page did not at first submit a design to Specification P.13/36 because of its existing contract to design and construct a twin-engined bomber to Specification B.1/35. Its design team was actively engaged in developing this large twin-Bristol Hercules bomber of 95ft wing span. Further investigation into the P.13/36 specification showed a marked similarity between the bomber designed to B.1/35 and one designed to P.13/36. All the B.1/35 requirements could be met by the P.13/36 bomber, with the exception of provision for a mid-upper gun turret. It was felt, however, that the heavier nose and tail turret armament of the P.13/36 would more than make up for the deletion of the upper turret. (In later years, of course, the mid-upper turret was incorporated on the P.13/36 designs). The Handley Page project team, under G. R. Volkert, found that the increased cruising speed required from the P.13/36 could be met by reducing the wing span to 90ft, and, in consequence, the wing area from 1,070sq ft to 975sq ft. This meant an increase in wing loading from 24.6lb/sq ft to 27.5lb/sq ft maximum on normal load.

Handley Page considered that the Rolls-Royce Vulture engine would not be available in fully developed form for some years, and proposed that its P.13/36 design should have two stages of engine installation. The first stage design would have two Bristol Hercules

Above right: Two views of the second prototype Manchester, L7247, in June 1940 soon after its maiden flight. Note the central 'shark's fin' – later replaced by a stronger broad chord one – and the fully extended Frazer-Nash FN21A ventral turret. Eventually the span was increased by almost 10ft.

Right: In August 1940 the first prototype Manchester, now basically in initial production model form, was allotted to the RAE Farnborough for various test purposes including catapult-assisted take-off trials.

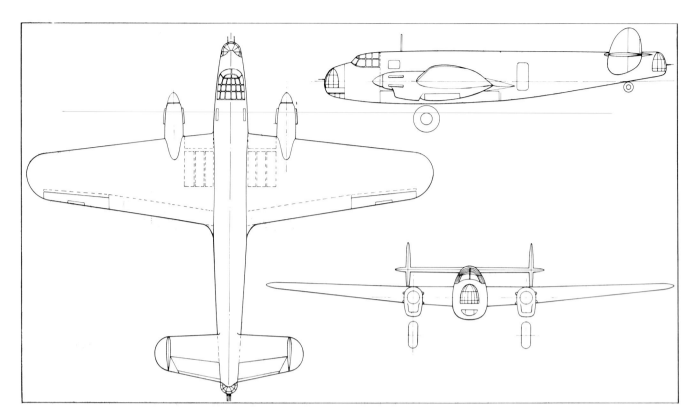

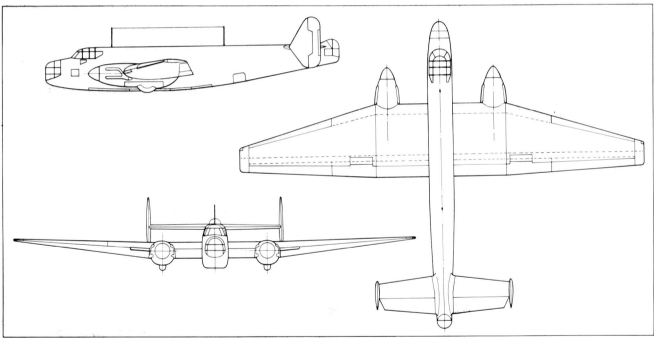

Top: The Hawker P.13/36 twin-engined bomber, powered by Rolls-Royce Vulture 24-cylinder in-line engines. Hawker's bomber had a wing span of 87ft and a length of 72ft 8in. It was not accepted for prototype development.

Above: Handley Page's design to meet the requirements of Specification P.13/36, powered by two Rolls-Royce Vulture engines. Wing radiators were intended to be installed, the outlet flaps for which can be seen on the plan view. This 90ft span monoplane, known by the company designation HP56, was redesigned with four Rolls-Royce Merlins, under the type number HP57, to become the Halifax.

Above right: The Handley Page Halifax Mk I, the first prototype of which, L7244, was initially flown without turrets. L7245, the second prototype, was similar in most respects to the production Mk I. The Halifax Mk I had a wing span of 98ft 10in and a length of 70ft 1in.

Right: The first prototype (unarmed) Handley Page Halifax, L7244, seen with its leading edge slats extended.

engines, like the B.1/35, with a cruising speed of 230mph. The second stage would have the Vulture engine installation, with which the cruising speed would increase to 275mph. It was considered that this change of engine could easily be brought about if the engine nacelles were designed from the outset to install either type of engine. It was suggested that if a development contract was placed the first prototype should have Hercules engines and the second Vultures. On September 22, 1936, Handley Page sent a formal letter to the Air Ministry requesting cancellation of its B.1/35 design contract, and replacement by a contract for a P.13/36 design, which would also meet the old B.1/35 requirements.

A similar letter, suggesting abandoning the B.1/35 and concentrating on the B.12/36 and P.13/36 designs was sent to the Air Ministry by Armstrong Whitworth.

On January 23, 1937, a letter was sent to Handley Page and Armstrong Whitworth from the Air Ministry stating that the aeroplanes designed to Specification B.1/35 were no longer required, and it was requested that all work on these designs should stop. Armstrong Whitworth wanted to work on the B.12/36 bomber, but was not permitted to owing to its commitments on

the P.27/32 light bomber and F.9/35 twin-engined fighter.

Handley Page received a new contract to design and develop two prototypes of its P.13/36 design. Evidently the Air Ministry did not share Handley Page's confidence regarding the availability of the Vulture engine and ordered the two prototypes of the HP56, as the new bomber was designated, to be powered by Rolls-Royce Vultures.

The new Handley Page aircraft was a mid-wing monoplane with a wing span of 90ft. It was of more angular appearance than the Avro P.13/36, but otherwise similar in performance and general layout. The front power-operated turret housed two .303in Browning guns and the rear turret four of these weapons. The turrets were designed and manufactured by Boulton Paul. To guard against side attacks, each side of the fuselage had an opening hatch, with hand-operated Vickers K guns. Most of the bomb load was carried in the capacious, unobstructed fuselage bay, with additional bomb cells between the fuselage and nacelles in the wing centre section.

After detail design was well advanced and construction had begun, the future of the Vulture engine gave

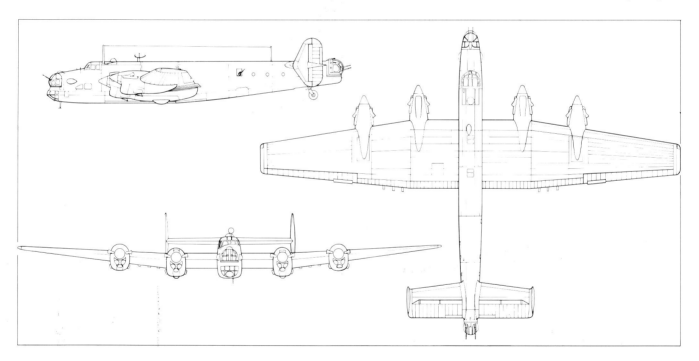

The second prototype Halifax, L7245, pictured at the A & AEE Boscombe Down in 1941 together with an early production Manchester I./*The Aeroplane*

rise to concern. It was proving more difficult to develop than at first seemed likely, with continual problems. There also had always been a substantial body of opinion within the Air Staff that favoured the use of four engines in the P.13/36 designs, but this had bee' overruled in favour of using two big engines – mainly because a smaller aircraft would result and maintenance problems would be eased. Difficulties with the Vulture and the lack of alternative engines in the same power class at a similar stage of development caused the Air Ministry to reconsider the engine layout of the HP56. Handley Page was asked to redesign the bomber with four Rolls-Royce Merlins, which meant considerable delay to the programme and a substantial increase in weight of the aircraft. Wing span was increased to 98ft 10in and fuselage length to 69ft 9in.

The redesigned bomber was given the works number HP57 and the original serial numbers of the two

HP56s, L7244 and L7245 were transferred to it. Later, the name Halifax I was bestowed on the aircraft and an initial production contract placed, although the latter was not confirmed until the beginning of January 1939. The first prototype, like the first Avro 679, was not fitted with gun turrets, but was at first fitted with automatic slats on the outer wings. These were deleted from the production-type Halifax because of the need to apply de-icing equipment and balloon-cable cutters.

Construction of the HP57 prototype began in 1938 and it was completed by the early autumn of 1939. Normally, all new Handley Page aeroplanes made their first flights from Radlett, but Britain was now at war and, in any case, the new classes of bombers being developed were secret. L7244, the first prototype, was therefore transferred in sections to RAF Bicester for assembly and flight trials. It was ready for flight in October, and on the 25th of that month Major J. Cordes, Handley Page's chief test pilot, took the new bomber into the air for the first time. The flight tests that followed confirmed the impressions gained on the first flight that the new aircraft was promising, and that no major changes would be needed on production aircraft.

The second prototype, L7245, fully-equipped with gun turrets, joined the test programme on August 17, 1940. This was followed by the first production Halifax I, L9485, which first flew on October 11, 1940.

The Halifax I had a loaded weight of 55,000lb, and an empty weight of 33,860lb, and could carry a maximum bomb load of 13,000lb for 1,000 miles, and a 5,800lb bomb load for 1,860 miles. Maximum speed was 262mph at 17,750ft. The nose turret housed two .303in Browning guns, the tail turret housed four of these weapons, and there was an opening hatch on each side of the fuselage through which a single Vickers K gun could be fired, each of these guns being manually-operated.

Most of the characteristics of the Halifax in relation to performance and load carrying ability came close to the figures laid down in Specification P.13/36, except for speed. In practice both the Manchester and Halifax cruised at around the 220mph figure originally called for when the specification was being drawn up, but considered in discussion to be too slow. Experience seemed to confirm that a cruising speed of around 200-230mph was the highest that could be achieved with a large bomber using either four engines in the 1,000hp class or two engines in the 2,000hp class, and still having good bomb load/range figures. In later years increases in engine power generally permitted the big bomber to maintain these cruising speeds whilst allowing increases in all-up weight caused by additional equipment being installed to make such aircraft more effective operationally.

The flight test programme of the production Halifax I was comparatively trouble-free and at this stage major changes to the aircraft were unnecessary. In November 1940 35 Squadron was re-formed at Linton-on-Ouse, Yorkshire, to become the first Halifax unit. That month, L7244, the first prototype, was lent to the squadron to give it experience of the new bomber. Shortly afterwards, the first operational production aircraft were delivered, among them L9486, the second production aircraft. The rest of 1940 was spent in training and familiarisation with the new aircraft, and it was not until the early part of 1941 that operations began.

Specification P.13/36 was probably the most significant requirement for a new bomber issued to the aircraft industry prior to the war. From it stemmed the Lancaster and Halifax, Bomber Command's two most important heavy bombers during the war years. By an unforeseen stroke of good fortune, the requirement for the aircraft to carry two torpedoes and the consequential need for a large unobstructed bomb bay, meant that the P.13/36 designs were able to accommodate some of the larger bombs that were to come into service without major redesign of the bomb bay.

The Bristol P.13/36 twin-Bristol Hercules-powered medium bomber. With a wing span of 79ft and an overall length of 55ft 9in this project was one of the smallest of the P.13/26 designs. The front turret design, housing two Browning guns, mounted through a thin rotating ring, was similar in design to that used on the Bristol Bombay production version (which used a single Vickers K gun). The rear turret mounted four Browning guns in a unique rotating ring, with 1,000 rounds per gun also stowed in the ring. The aircraft carried a maximum bomb load of 8,000lb, had a top speed of 315mph at 15,000ft at an all-up weight of 22,000lb, and had a range of 2,000 miles carrying 2,500lb of bombs.

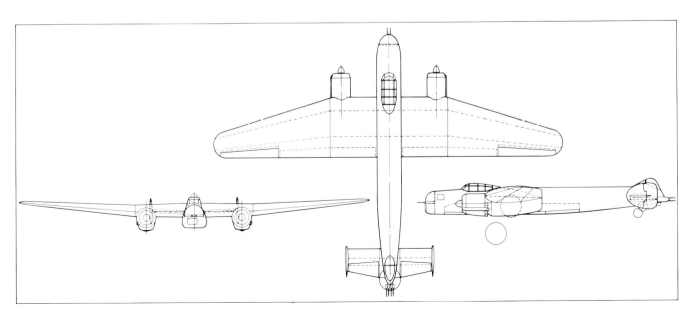

Aeroplanes for the Squadrons

Production of the Vickers Wellesley, Handley Page Harrow, Armstrong Whitworth Whitley, Bristol Blenheim, Fairey Battle, Handley Page Hampden and Vickers Wellington gets under way.

One of the most pressing needs in the expanding RAF was the rapid training of a great number of aircrew of all grades. This was particularly necessary in the case of Bomber Command: many new medium and heavy bomber squadrons were planned and each aircraft in a squadron had several crew members. It was considered that the best way to achieve this result was to select a well-tried type of bomber, produce it in large numbers, and equip the newly-formed squadrons with the type to provide operational training until sufficient numbers of the new monoplanes became available in quantity.

To this end the Hawker Hind, a refined development of the excellent, well-established Hart biplane light bomber, was produced in large numbers to provide equipment for the new squadrons. The adoption of the Hind made such good sense despite the single-engined biplane's obsolescence: the Hart was already well-established in service and it had proved to be an out-standing aircraft. Also it was, in its various versions, still in production and the similar Hind would not cause major disruption of the production lines. Furthermore the Flying Training Schools were already using the Hart Trainer for extensive training of bomber pilots, with a Hind trainer version also on order. There would thus be a continuation of training after a pilot left Flying Training School and joined an operational squadron, where he would be flying an aircraft already familiar to him.

The first Hart Trainers had been delivered to the

RAF College at Cranwell and to operational fighter squadrons during 1933. Subsequently, they had been the subject of large orders and the type was, by 1936, in use at all the major Flying Training Schools in very large numbers. The Hart bomber had been in service with operational squadrons since 1930.

Designed to meet the requirements of Specification G.7/34, the Hind prototype, K2915, had first flown on September 12, 1934 and the first production Hind followed a year later, on September 4, 1935. Powered, in the bomber version, by a 640hp Rolls-Royce Kestrel V, the Hind had a top speed of 188mph and could carry a maximum bomb load of 510lb.

The Hind Trainer was powered by the 599hp Kestrel VDR, but although lower powered it attained a similar top speed to that of the bomber version, due to its lower all-up weight. Due to the re-positioning of the centre of gravity caused by the removal of armament

and other military equipment, the Hart and Hind trainers only had two and a half degrees of sweepback on their upper wings instead of the normal five degrees of the majority of Hart/Hind variants. By the end of 1936, eighteen squadrons had re-equipped with Hinds. Harts from squadrons newly re-equipped with Hinds became the equipment of seven Auxiliary Air Force squadrons by the end of 1936. By the beginning of 1937 some 300 Hinds and around 100 Harts were on the strength of Bomber Command, and these provided training for large numbers of aircrew members in preparation for the advanced new types about to enter service.

Another general-purpose bomber biplane that con-

A Hawker Hart Trainer of 10 FTS, Ternhill, Salop, in July 1938. Note blind flying hood (folded) on rear cockpit.

tinued in production during 1936 was the Westland Wallace, the last leaving the Westland factory in October 1936. The Wallace, developed from the earlier Wapiti, was the last biplane in production that retained a direct link with World War I design. The earlier Wapiti was the winner of a competition to find a successor to the DH9A, and in accordance with the requirements of the specification it utilised standard DH9A components where possible – in this case, wings and tailplane. Later Wapitis, whilst retaining DH9A basic wing and tailplane geometry, used a fully-metallised structure. The same wings and tail unit, married to a new wider fuselage, produced the Wallace. In 1936 the version of the Wallace still in production was the Mk II. The Wallace was, of course, outdated as a front-line bomber, but it did provide useful training for the pilots of the Auxiliary squadrons. No 501 Squadron retained its Mk Is until 1936 and No 502 flew the Mk II until April 1937. Nos 503 and 504 Squadrons flew Wallaces until June 1936 and May 1937 respectively. By the summer of 1937 the Wallaces had been replaced by Harts or Hinds in all these squadrons.

Of all the Air Ministry specifications for new types issued to the aircraft industry, it is probable that G.4/31, issued to develop a new general purpose aircraft to replace the Wapiti, Vildebeest and Vincent, produced a greater variety of individual prototypes than any other. Eventually, after the evaluation of many prototypes, the private venture Vickers single-engined monoplane was selected for production. Built by Vickers to provide a comparison between their official biplane entry in the G.4/31 competition and their private venture ideas utilising a monoplane wing of high aspect ratio married to the fuselage and tail

unit of the G.4/31 biplane, their monoplane confirmed the superiority of this type of layout.

So superior was the Vickers G.4/31 monoplane over all its rivals that it was adopted over all the official entries and Vickers were awarded a contract for 96 production models. The contract, under a new specification, 22/35, was issued in September 1935 and the aircraft was to be known as the Wellesley. The rest of 1935 and the whole of 1936 (in which year 80 more Wellesleys were ordered) was spent in redesigning the Wellesley for production and setting up the production line at Weybridge. Owing to the urgent need to re-equip the bomber squadrons with modern monoplanes, the initial batches of Wellesleys were selected to equip some of the home-based units – including a number of squadrons newly-formed under the Expansion Scheme. The first production Wellesley, K7713, made its first flight on January 30, 1937, and the type entered squadron service, with No 76 Squadron at Finningley, Yorkshire, in April of that year.

Specification B.3/34 resulted in production orders for two types of twin-engined heavy night bomber to replace the existing ageing twin-engined biplanes, the Virginia and Heyford. Of these two new monoplanes, one was intended as an interim aircraft which would be useful in training crews to handle bombers of modern configuration, and which could be passed on to fulfil the transport role after it had been replaced by more modern bomber types, while the other was a poten-

Westland Wallace IIs of 502 (Ulster) Squadron, a Special Reserve unit in 6 (Auxiliary) Group, Bomber Command, which operated from Aldergrove in Northern Ireland.

The pre-production Vickers Wellesley, K7556, pictured on take-off.

tially more advanced aircraft capable of development, and one which was to form the future backbone of the night striking force.

The interim twin-engined bomber was the Handley Page 54, which was ordered 'off the drawing board' and into production without awaiting the usual prototype trials. One hundred aircraft of this type were ordered under the name Harrow, to a revised specification, B.29/35. The aircraft's performance and flying qualities could be predicted with confidence because the design was based on an earlier Handley Page aeroplane, the HP51 bomber-transport. The Harrow was considerably 'cleaner' and less angular than its progenitor. Both were high-wing monoplanes with a monoplane tailplane and twin fins and rudders. The Harrow had a wing span of 88ft 5in compared with 90ft of the HP51. The revised tail unit for the Harrow was first flown on the HP51.

For production the Harrow structure was one of the first in this country to be broken down into small components for ease of manufacture. Up to this point it had been customary to build such major components as the mainplane or fuselage in one piece. Handley Page concluded that it would be advantageous to produce a number of smaller components, to be assembled eventually on a final assembly jig to complete the major

component of, say, the mainplane or fuselage. This method speeded production by permitting the smaller components to be sub-contracted to firms with a small labour force and it also permitted larger numbers of workers to work on one major component at the same time without congestion. It also had advantages for the repair of damage to a major component. 'Split construction', as it was initially called, soon became the normal method of producing aeroplanes in large quantities, but the Harrow structure certainly pioneered the method in this country.

Although it was considered likely that the Harrow would soon be replaced in the squadrons by more advanced types, the big Handley Page bomber was a modern aircraft in most respects and gave invaluable training to bomber crews in the methods of operating the new types of long-range high-performance monoplanes. Its cruising speed of 163mph on 54 per cent max power (500hp per engine) at 15,000ft was some 60mph higher than the Heyford and 90mph higher than that of the Virginia. The first 39 Harrows were

63

Mk Is, not fully-operational aircraft, which were issued to squadrons to familiarise crews with the new monoplane bomber. The Mk I was powered by two 850hp Bristol Pegasus X engines which gave a top speed of 190mph and a cruising speed of 154mph at 15,000ft. The fully-equipped Mk II, powered by two 925hp Bristol Pegasus XX engines, had a top speed of 200mph and a cruising speed of 163mph.

One important advance brought into general use with the Harrow was the installation of front, mid-upper, and rear power-operated defensive armament. Single Lewis guns were normally used in the front and mid-upper turrets, but the rear turret housed a pair of these weapons. In the design of the front and rear turrets the main glazing was fixed, with only a transparent ring, through which the guns projected, rotating. Power-operated turrets had previously only been installed in the Overstrands of 101 Squadron, and then in the front position only. Mk I Harrows did not have the turrets installed when first delivered to the squadrons, but many were retrospectively fitted later.

The Harrow's entire bomb load (3,000lb max) was stowed internally in a fuselage bay.

The undercarriage of the Harrow was fixed; it was considered that the slight extra gain in speed resulting from a retractable undercarriage would not justify the complete redesign of the HP51 layout to a mid-wing. This would have been necessary in order to shorten the undercarriage leg for retraction into the nacelles. This complete change of layout would have altered the flying characteristics so much that construction of a prototype would have been advisable before commencing production. This would have delayed the introduction of the Harrow into service by at least a year, and the aircraft was urgently required.

The Harrow's wing design embodied advanced aerodynamic technology combining a highly-tapered planform with special high lift devices, such as large leading edge slats and large flaps. These enabled the big bomber to take off from small grass airfields with full load. When its days as a first-line bomber ended the Harrow gave invaluable service as a squadron transport and casualty evacuation aircraft. In the latter role it was the only big aeroplane that could land and take-off from small makeshift landing grounds to evacuate wounded from battle zones.

It has been stated in some publications that when used as a transport the Harrow was reverting to the role for which it was originally designed, and that it was hastily adapted as a bomber. This is not the case: the Harrow was designed from the outset as a heavy bomber, with troop-carrying and general transport as a

Left: A batch of six Wellesleys, complete with under-wing bomb containers, on the airfield at Vickers' Weybridge works early in 1938 ready for delivery to the RAF.

Below left: Close-up of one of the two detachable under-wing bomb containers of a Wellesley; each container could accommodate a 1,000lb bomb load. In service, some vibration was experienced when diving the Wellesley with the container doors open but this was eventually cured by removing the doors, with little influence on drag.

Below: Big stick from Marham. A Handley Page Harrow II (K6962, originally built as a Mk I) of 115 Squadron. Note single gun in dorsal turret and twin guns in tail turret.

secondary role. It was, however, based on the design of a bomber-transport, as the class was traditionally called, the Handley Page 51. The HP51 was designed to the Specification C.26/31, the successful contender for which was the Bristol Bombay. It is ironic to note that although the Bombay was selected in preference to the HP51 for production, the Harrow, the HP51's direct descendant, in fact proved to be more universally used than the Bristol bomber-transport in that role.

The Handley Page Harrow is also noteworthy as the first production type to be finished in the newly-adopted camouflage scheme of Dark Green and Dark Earth on the upper surfaces, with Night (black) undersides. This is related elsewhere in the section on camouflage schemes.

The first production Harrow, K6933, which was also used for development flying, was completed at the beginning of October 1936, and made its first flight on the 10th of that month. Production build-up was rapid, and by April 1937 the Harrow was ready to enter service with the RAF.

The second heavy night bomber designed to Specification B.3/34 was the Armstrong Whitworth Whitley, which, as related in chapter 2, had been completed in prototype form and flown on March 17, 1936. Like the Harrow the design of the Whitley was greatly assisted by aerodynamic knowledge gained from a contender for the C.26/31 specification competition, in this case the Armstrong Whitworth AW23. As a contract for 80 Whitleys had been signed in June 1935, well before the first flight of the prototype, production of the new night bomber was able to commence. By March 1937 the first production Whitley I was flown, with further aircraft from the production line following rapidly. Acceptance trials progressed smoothly and the first Whitley I reached 10 Squadron at Dishforth, Yorks, on March 9.

The Whitley I, powered by two 795hp Armstrong-Siddeley Tiger IX engines, had a similar performance to the Harrow – cruising at 160mph at 16,000ft and having a top speed of 192mph. At 160mph it could carry 3,350lb of bombs for 1,650 miles. Over short ranges it could carry the heavy bomb load, for its day, of 7,000lb. The Whitley I carried single Lewis guns in the front and rear manually-operated turret, with provision for a ventral 'dustbin' retractable turret. Dihedral was added to the outer mainplanes, which became one of the characteristic features of the Whitley, after completion of a small number. The initial production Whitley Is were virtually identical to the prototype, K4586, and to the second prototype, K4587, which was completed early in 1937. Production of the Whitley I continued throughout 1937, with a total of 34 being completed.

The structure of the Whitley was a major technical advance on all previous heavy night bombers ordered for the RAF. The fuselage and nacelles were entirely constructed of metal, with metal skinning. The wing was built on the monospar principle, with all the strength loads being taken on a single massive box spar, constructed of corrugated webs. The upper and lower web plates formed part of the aerofoil section of the wing and the box spar thus extended to the full depth of the wing. The wing fuel tanks were located along the leading edge of the inner wing outboard of the nacelles; they formed part of the aerofoil section and were attached to the front of the box spar. All the leading edge forward of the box spar was constructed of metal with metal skins. The aft part of the wing, which

Whitley Is of 10 Squadron at Dishforth, Yorks, first squadron to be armed with the type./*Flight International*

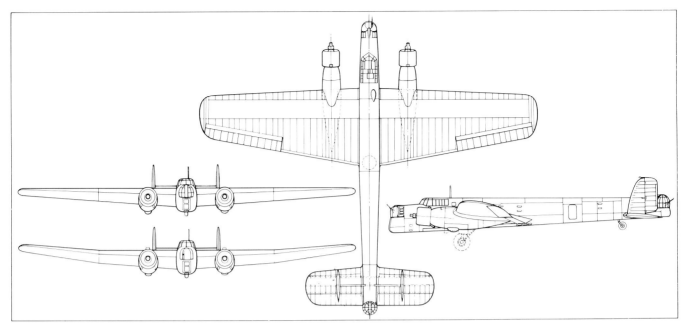

The Armstrong Whitworth Whitley III, powered by Armstrong Siddeley Tiger VIII fourteen-cylinder radial engines. Whitley III night bombers were used operationally during the early months of the war, flying deep into enemy territory on leaflet dropping raids. The span of the Whitley III was 84ft and the length was 69ft 3in. The height was 15ft. The first production Whitley Is did not have dihedral on the outer wings.

contained bomb cells in the inner sections, was constructed of metal, with fabric covering. The tail unit of the Whitley was an all-metal structure with fabric covering.

The main undercarriage units retracted forwards into the nacelles, with a small portion of each retracted wheel exposed. The tail wheel was fixed in the down position.

The main load of heavy bombs was carried in the fuselage bay, but smaller bombs were carried in the wing cells. Small practice bombs could be accommodated in the small bay aft of the ventral turret position. The largest bomb which could be stowed in the main bomb bay was the 2,000lb armour-piercing weapon.

While production of the Mk I gained momentum development of the Whitley continued. Re-engining the aircraft with the 920hp Tiger VIII gave an improved performance, and this version was known as the Whitley II and followed the Mk I on the production lines. This improved Whitley, produced to Specification B.21/35, had a maximum speed at sea level of 185mph and 215mph at 15,000ft. Cruising at 177mph at 15,000ft and carrying a bomb load of 3,365lb the Whitley II had a range of 1,315 miles. Forty-six were built, delivery commencing in January 1938.

Further development of the Tiger-engined Whitley resulted in the Mk III, built to Specification B.20/36. The main changes in this mark were the replacement of the manually-operated Armstrong Whitworth nose turret, with its single Lewis or Vickers K gun, by a power-operated Vickers K gun-armed Nash and Thompson turret and the addition of a retractable ventral 'dustbin' turret equipped with two .303 Browning guns. Another change concerning armament was that the bomb bays and racks were now capable of accommodating bigger bombs. A modified Mk I, K7211, served as the prototype Mk III, and altogether

80 production aircraft were built, beginning with K8936; they were delivered during the latter half of 1938. Powerplant of the Whitley III was again the Tiger VIII and its performance was the same as that of the Mk II.

So swift was the pace of combat aircraft development in the late 1930s that the Whitley III was close to being obsolescent even when deliveries first began. But already the Whitley had gained a new lease of life following the decision to re-engine the type with Rolls-Royce Merlins. The first Merlin-powered Whitley to fly (on February 11, 1938) was the modified Mk I, K7208, this test aircraft later being joined by two more converted Mk Is, K7209 and K7211. Thus was born the Whitley IV (commencing K9016) which, apart from the engines, the propellers, and the Plexiglass 'chin' extension replacing the old hinged door-type bomb-aimer's window, was outwardly identical to the Mk III. Among the internal changes that were made was the installation of two extra fuel tanks in the wings.

Powered by two 1,030hp Merlin IV engines, the Whitley IV had a markedly improved performance. Top speed was 244mph at 16,400ft and cruising speed 220mph at 15,000ft. Maximum range was 1,800 miles and normal range, with a maximum bomb load of 3,365lb, was 1,250 miles. A total of 33 Mk IVs were built, beginning with K9016, plus seven Mk IVAs powered by 1,070hp Merlin Xs.

Development of the Whitley IV led to the Mk V,

most extensively produced version of all – although in common with many other bombers it was, of course, eventually adapted for other duties outside its principal sphere of activity. Powered by two Merlin Xs, like the Whitley IVA, the Mk V introduced a Nash and Thompson rear turret mounting four .303in Browning guns, thereby becoming the first bomber in the world to be so powerfully armed against attack from astern. At the same time the rear fuselage was extended by 15in to give the rear gunner a wider field of fire on the beam. The two-gun ventral turret was discarded but the single-gun Nash and Thompson nose turret was retained. Other innovations on the Mk V included modified fins with straight leading edges, additional fuel tanks to increase the normal capacity (a further increase again being possible by carrying auxiliary tanks in the bomb bay) and rubber de-icing boots on the leading edges of the wings.

Serving as a trials aircraft for the 4-gun Nash and Thompson rear turret was Whitley I K7183 which was modified in April 1939 and tested in May. The first Whitley V, N1345, first flew on August 8, 1939, and the type was just entering service when war was declared.

In 1933 the Bristol Aeroplane Company designed a twin-engined, low-wing, cabin monoplane to carry six passengers and a crew of two. It was to be powered by Bristol Aquila engines and the fuselage was exhibited at the 1934 Paris Aero Show. The aircraft was brought to the attention of Lord Rothermere, who, after examining the full specification, ordered a revised version for use as an executive transport. The resulting aircraft, known as the Bristol Type 142, employed similar wing and tail but had a fuselage of reduced cross-sectional area to reduce drag. The new transport seated five in comfort, and was operated by a crew of two. To increase performance the Type 142 was powered by two 640hp Bristol Mercury VI engines instead of Aquilas, and a top speed of at least 250mph was expected.

The Type 142 made its first flight on April 12, 1935, and in subsequent trials proved to have an outstanding performance. Its high speed and modern design aroused the interest of the Air Staff, who were currently concerned with developing a new generation of day bombers to replace the ageing biplanes, and, at the end of May the Chief of the Air Staff wrote ' . . . I agree, also, that the Bristol twin should be considered as a medium bomber if Bristols have a reasonable proposition to put forward for the supply of this type in reasonable numbers. In this connection I suggest that we should offer to test the aircraft made for Lord Rothermere at Martlesham free of charge in order to ascertain its performance and characteristics. This offer should be made to the company and they should obtain the assent of Lord Rothermere if such is necessary'. Not only was Lord Rothermere agreeable to the tests, but presented the aircraft to the Air Council. He named it *Britain First*.

At Martlesham Heath, wearing roundels and the

Above: Whitley IVs on the production line together with a solitary Tiger-powered machine (the latter apparently undergoing repair) at Armstrong Whitworth's Baginton factory in April 1939.

Right: The installation of a four-gun Nash and Thompson tail turret in the new Whitley V in 1939 gave that aircraft the most effective rearwards defence of any heavy bomber then extant.

serial K7557, the Type 142 was seen to have a speed of 285mph at maximum loaded weight and a top speed of 307mph, which was considerably more than the fastest contemporary fighters. By July 1935 Bristols had proposed a bomber variant, the Type 142 M, with the wing moved to the mid-position to allow space for a bomb bay and with a mid-upper gun turret. By August Specification B.28/35 had been drawn up to cover the project, and a contract was placed for 150 of the new bombers under the Type name Blenheim I. The Blenheim I was thus ordered 'straight off the drawing board' without waiting for prototype development, the Type 142 giving sufficient indication of the new bomber's characteristics. Less than a year later, on June 25, 1936, the first Blenheim I off the production line at Filton, Bristol, K7033, made its first flight.

Blenheim production was now put in hand at two other main centres on a sub-contract basis. In October 1936 a contract was placed with Rootes Securities Ltd at Speke (near Liverpool), under the Shadow Factory Scheme, for 336 Blenheim Is and in February 1937 a contract for 250 was placed with Avro. The last-named company built the aircraft in the then new shadow factory at Chadderton (near Manchester) which was handed over to it by the Government in 1938. Such was the urgency of the RAF Expansion Programme that construction was actually begun at Chadderton before the buildings were complete.

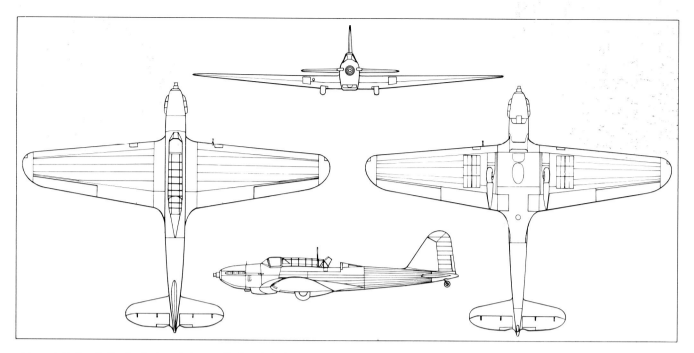

Above left: The Bolingbroke I prototype with its original nose.

Left: A Filton-built Blenheim IV on test, showing to advantage the mark's characteristic lengthened and scalloped nose./*Bristol Aeroplane Co*

Above: The Fairey Battle I, developed from the P.27/32 prototype, K4303. An interesting aerodynamic feature of the Battle was the offset fin and rudder, with a cambered aerofoil section. Another feature of the Battle was the very deep root wing section and thin tip.

airliner, under the type name Hudson, to fill the gap before the Beaufort and Botha were available, and to replace the Avro Anson in the general reconnaissance role. The Bolingbroke general reconnaissance aircraft was therefore abandoned, but as the improved 'long-nose' Blenheim incorporated all the modifications requested by RAF bomber squadrons after experience of operating the Blenheim I the new version was placed in production under the type name Blenheim IV. Eventually the Blenheim IV replaced the Mk I on the production lines.

The name Bolingbroke was subsequently revived for a version of the Blenheim IV produced in Canada. Some Blenheim IVs operated in Coastal Command in later years, in the general reconnaissance role, as well as for shipping strikes. The first deliveries of the Blenheim IV were made from Filton in February 1938 and thereafter production built up from the three production lines at Filton, Speke, and Manchester. By the outbreak of war on September 3, 1939, about 130 Mk IV bombers had been delivered to the RAF.

Fairey's successful P.24/32 design, the Battle, was another of the types selected for mass production under the Shadow Factory Scheme. The initial order, for 155 Battles conforming to Specification P.23/35, was placed with the parent company in 1935. In 1936, the year in which the first prototype made its maiden flight,

additional orders were placed with Fairey to Specification P.14/36 and with Austin Motors to Specification P.32/36. The Fairey production line was in the new factory at Heaton Chapel, Stockport, – although the first production Battle, K7558, was built at Hayes – and the Austin order for 863 aircraft, a massive order for those days, was to be executed at that company's Longbridge (Birmingham) factory and later at Elmdon, Birmingham's airport.

The production Battle differed from K4303, the prototype, in its initial form, in several respects. The original Fairey-Reed fixed-pitch three-bladed propeller was replaced by a de Havilland variable-pitch three-blader, the open exhaust ports of the prototype in its original form gave way to kidney-type exhaust manifolds, and the long, glazed canopy was revised in design. Internally, full operational equipment was added. All these changes had previously been made to K4303, which was brought up to production standard, and in this form it was demonstrated at the 1936 RAF Display at Hendon. The modifications made to the basic design to turn it into an operational combat aeroplane made the Battle less 'clean' aerodynamically. The de Havilland propeller, due to its variable-pitch operating mechanism, would have required a larger spinner than that originally fitted when the Fairey-Reed propeller was installed. As this would have necessitated a complete redesign of the nose contours, the resulting delay in production was considered unacceptable. The DH propeller was therefore installed without a spinner, with only minor changes to the engine cowling.

The production changes reduced the Battle's top speed from 257mph to 243mph at 16,200ft when powered by the Rolls-Royce Merlin I engine. The installation of the 1,440hp Merlin III engine tended to restore the performance to some extent, but during the

Battle's testing time in France during 1939 and 1940 its low top and cruising speeds, together with the light defensive armament of one fixed .303in Browning gun operated by the pilot and one .303in Vickers K gun for rear defence, proved to be totally inadequate when intercepted by opposing fighters.

The first production Battle, K7558, was completed in the spring of 1937, and the first Battle delivered to a RAF squadron, No 63 at Upwood, was K7559. This, the second production Battle, was received on May 20, 1937. Thereafter production and deliveries steadily built up and in July 1938 the first Battle from the second production source, L4935, at Austin Motors at Longbridge, was completed. Eventually, 2,185 Battles were produced, albeit many of them for non-operational roles.

Although the Battle rapidly became obsolete it made an important contribution to the build-up of trained bomber crews – although unfortunately many of these were lost during the Battle of France. The Battle continued to train bomber crews under the Empire Training Scheme and it made a significant contribution to future RAF equipment when a number of Battles were converted to test fly various new high-powered engines of all types. These Battles test flew such engines as the Bristol Hercules, Bristol Centaurus, Rolls-Royce Vulture, Rolls-Royce Exe, Rolls-Royce Griffon, Fairey P.12, and Napier Sabre, contributing much to speeding development of these engines – many of which were to play an all-important part in maintaining the high performance of RAF aircraft.

First test-flown during 1936, Handley Page's B.9/32 twin-engined bomber, the HP52, had to await completion of the order for 100 Harrows before production could begin. While preparations for production of the HP52 under the type name Hampden I were being made the design office was engaged in redesigning the bomber to make improvements and alterations to increase its efficiency. Some of these changes were made in the light of test flight results and others to introduce war equipment.

Flight trials of the two HP52 prototypes, K4240 and L7271, had indicated a need to improve lateral stability and to achieve this, dihedral was incorporated on the outer wing panels of the production Hampden. The two 1,000hp Bristol Pegasus XVIII radial engines were mounted further forward from the wing leading edge.

Armament changes were effected by the design office when preparing the Hampden for production. When first flown K4240 had a Heyford 'dustbin'-type ventral turret built into the fuselage below the trailing edge, but this was found to cause drag problems. This was soon replaced by a more smoothly faired glazed position, with a manually-operated Vickers K gun installed. The mid-upper Vickers K gun was installed in an open position, which had a fully-glazed hemispherical canopy. This completely enclosed the gun

position when closed and with the gun stowed away, but it also acted as a large windshield for the gunner when folded in the open position. The top contours of the fuselage were altered to match this new, enlarged fairing.

The front armament and bomb-aimer's position was the subject of several design studies before a final production solution was evolved. The first of these envisaged a similar arrangement of front defensive guns as in the Harrow, with a deep fixed, glazed front gun position, with power-operated guns rotating and elevating through a movable glazed ring. Another design study favoured a similar gun arrangement, but with a separate glazed chin fairing for the bomb-aimer – as later used on the Handley Page Halifax I. These turrets would inevitably have caused a lowering of performance, due to drag increases.

As the Hampden possessed a high performance it seemed only right to extract the highest possible speeds out of it, and to this end it was considered better to redesign the front fuselage around smooth low-drag contours. The thoughts of installing power-operated front guns gave way to a fixed .303in Browning gun for the pilot and one movable Vickers K gun, also of .303in calibre, operated by the bomb-aimer and having a limited arc of fire. The extreme front of the streamlined nose was glazed, with an optically flat panel for the bomb aimer.

Larger diameter wheels were installed on production Hampdens to cope with the increase in weight over the prototype.

The first production Hampden, L4032, was completed in May 1938. Like the Harrow the Hampden was constructed on 'split assembly' methods, which speeded production. Test flying of the new bomber progressed smoothly, and the first squadron to be equipped with the Hampden, No 49 at Scampton, received its first on September 20, 1938, and had been fully armed with the type by the end of November. 83 Squadron began to receive Hampdens during November 1938 and 50 followed suit during December. Thereafter steady deliveries from Handley Page's Radlett and Cricklewood factories were augmented by the opening of a new production line at English Electric's Preston works. A third line was set up in Canada with the formation of Canadian Associated Aircraft Ltd, a group of companies brought together to sub-contract the Hampden. The first Canadian Hampden flew for the first time on August 9, 1940, and eventually 160 were produced. Total Handley Page production reached 500, the last flying in July 1940

Above right: A Fairey Battle (K7559) of No 63 Squadron, which in May 1937 became the first squadron to receive the type.

Right: Typical RAF Expansion Scheme factory scene – this one showing Battles in final assembly at the Austin shadow factory at Longbridge, Birmingham before the war.

74

when Hampden production ceased in favour of the Halifax. English Electric built 770 Hampdens under sub-contract between February 1940 and March 1942.

The production Hampden I, which was built to Specification 30/36, attained a top speed of 265mph at 15,500ft and 254mph at 13,800ft. Economical cruising speed was 167mph, which could be raised to 217mph if necessary. Maximum range with a 2,000lb bomb load was 1,990 miles. Maximum bomb load was 4,000lb, which could be carried for 870 miles.

Short and Harland at Belfast received an order for 100 (later increased to 150) versions of the Hampden powered by two Napier Dagger VIII 24-cylinder 'H' configuration engines. These aircraft were, apart from the engine installation, identical to the Pegasus-powered Hampden and they attained a similar performance – albeit possibly slightly higher at cruising power. The Dagger-powered version was evolved under Specification 44/36 and named Hereford I.

Problems arose with providing adequate cooling for the rear cylinders on the high-revving Dagger engines, and this, together with excessive engine noise causing fatigue in long flights, made the Hereford unsatisfactory and the total production order was not completed. Only one flight, in 185 Squadron – then a bomber operational training unit – was equipped with the Hereford and these were soon withdrawn.

The production-type Wellington evolved from design development of the Vickers B.1/35 Warwick heavy bomber. The Wellington's ancestor, the B.9/32, and the first B.1/35 studies had evolved in parallel from the earliest days of the Weybridge design team's first drafts of a bomber to meet the B.1/35 specification. To meet these requirements they stretched the original B.9/32 design by incorporating an integral parallel fuselage centre section and by extending the wing and tailplane.

The necessity to incorporate power-operated turrets

and a greatly increased bomb load led to a complete redesign of the fuselage of the B.1/35, which in turn could be used to advantage, albeit in shortened form, in the production version of the B.9/32. Further development of the geodetic structure by Dr Barnes Wallis made it possible to redesign the fuselage in less symmetrical form, with a revised cross-section which widened the lower part of the fuselage to permit more bombs to be stowed in the bomb bay. The bomb load requirements for the B.1/35 were in fact exceeded by a comfortable margin.

The B.1/35 armament requirement for power-operated turrets mounting one .303in calibre machine gun in the nose and two similar guns in the tail was met by Vickers-designed turrets contoured to the new fuselage shape. They each had a fixed glazed section, with sliding panels for the guns. These turrets were used on the Wellington I but were never installed in the B.1/35 prototypes. By the time the first B.1/35 was completed the Vickers turrets in both aircraft types had been replaced by Frazer-Nash turrets.

The cockpit of the B.9/32 had been covered by an angular, flat-panelled canopy and this had been the

Below: Handley Page Hampden I, the production development of the Handley Page B.9/32 (HP52) day bomber. One of the projected front fuselage designs considered for the production Hampden. The 'chin' bomb-aimer's window layout was later introduced on the Halifax.

Right: Service pilots collect brand new Hampdens from Handley Page's airfield at Radlett early in 1939. Note the standard single rear .303 guns in the upper and lower gun positions of Hampden L4113 in the foreground.

Below right: Newly-completed Handley Page Herefords, built by Shorts at Belfast, awaiting delivery in 1939. Due to the Dagger engines being extremely temperamental the Hereford's career was but brief, and many machines were eventually converted to Hampden configuration.

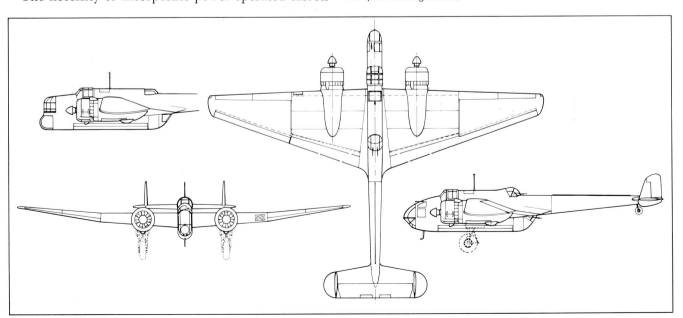

Composite Emergency Bomber

Birth of the Armstrong Whitworth Albemarle.

Early in 1938 the Air Staff gave their attention to the problem of evolving a useful medium bomber which could be quickly built in a time of national emergency by untrained or semi-skilled labour drawn from sources other than the aircraft industry. In this bomber the structural design was to make use of such materials as wood, metal, synthetic material and compressed laminated wood.

Discussions about the desired new bomber hardened into the issue of a Specification, B.9/38, to invite tenders from certain companies of the industry. Four companies were approached about the new specification, Avro, Handley Page, Bristol and Armstrong Whitworth. Avro and Handley Page, both heavily committed to bombers covered by Specification P.13/36, were not enthusiastic about the B.9/38 concept. Frank Barnwell, chief designer of Bristol, and John Lloyd, chief designer of Armstrong Whitworth, were, however, both deeply interested in the challenge represented by the new specification, and projected designs to meet the requirement.

The specification required the composite bomber to have a speed, at maximum economical cruising power, of not less than 300mph at 15,000ft. The range with 1,500lb of bombs at 15,000ft was to be not less than 1,500 miles with a maximum range without bombs of 3,000 miles. In overload condition a bomb load of 3,000lb was required to be carried for not less than 2,000 miles, again at 15,000ft.

A crew of four was to be carried, with provision for an additional pilot as a relief on long flights.

The bomb load was to consist of any of the following loads: 12 x 250lb, six 500lb bombs, six 250lb 'B' bombs, or two 2,000lb AP bombs. A four .303in gun turret was to be installed in the tail.

The issue of the specification evoked considerable comment from various sources close to the planning of future operational bomber types. The Deputy Chief of

the Air Staff suggested that it would be wiser to concentrate on the development of a general reconnaissance aircraft of composite construction, with bombing as a possible secondary role because the B.9/38 bomber was not likely to meet future Bomber Command requirements by the time it could be in service.

Frank Barnwell projected his composite bomber in two forms, one with conventional tail-down main undercarriage and the second with the then-new and untried tricycle undercarriage. The conventional undercarriage version resulted in an 80ft span aeroplane powered by two Hercules SM engines which should achieve a top speed of 302mph. The similarly-powered tricycle version had a span of 70ft and achieved an estimated top speed of 319mph. Bristol favoured the use of a conventional undercarriage because of improved general performance, despite the lower top speed.

The normal bomb load for both versions was 1,000lb, carried over 1,500 miles, but the range could be increased to 2,000 miles with the following loads: eight 500lb GP bombs, 10 x 250lb bombs, six 250lb Type 'B' bombs or two 2,000 AP bombs.

Although Specification B.9/38 called for a four-gun tail turret, Bristol favoured using a mid-upper and mid-lower turret arrangement, with two .303in Brownings in each turret. It was felt that this arrangement gave wide defensive protection from rear and beam attacks by providing an almost 360-degree arc of fire. A crew of five was specified.

John Lloyd at Armstrong Whitworth chose a mid-wing layout based on the power of two Rolls-Royce Merlin engines, with two Bristol Hercules engines as second choice. A further alternative was an installation of two Armstrong Siddeley Deerhound engines when these became available.

With Merlin engines the new project was estimated to carry 3,500lb of bombs for 2,500 miles, although normal load would be 1,500lb of bombs for 2,000 miles.

The Armstrong Whitworth design carried a crew of five, and defence was provided by a mid-upper turret housing four .303in Browning guns and a retractable

The prototype Armstrong Whitworth Albemarle, P1360, as first flown in 1940.

ventral turret housing two of these weapons. Lloyd designed his aircraft from the outset to have a tricycle undercarriage and, like the Bristol project with this type of landing gear, the wing span was about 70ft. The long fuselage bomb bay, enclosed by two spruce and plywood doors, could carry any of the following loads: nine 500lb GP bombs, 15 x 250lb GP bombs, six 250lb Type 'B' bombs, two 2,000lb AP bombs, or nine small bomb containers. For ferrying flights additional fuel tanks could be installed, instead of bombs, in the bomb bay, extending the estimated range to 4,000 miles. The nose section of the aircraft, constructed of non-magnetic stainless steel tubing and wood, housed the navigator in comfortable and light surroundings enhanced by extensive glazing. Optically flat panels in the extreme nose were provided for the bomb aimer. Twin fins and rudders were chosen to minimise interference with the arcs of fire of the turrets, fins and rudders sizes being kept as small as possible for this purpose.

The basic structure of the Armstrong Whitworth B.9/38 consisted of mixed wood, steel and duralumin components. The fuselage consisted of a tubular steel warren-girder box structure carrying fore and aft loads, attached to which were light spruce and plywood panels forming the contours. The wing loads were carried through a massive tubular steel warren girder 'box' spar, which ran from wing tip to wing tip, and integrated with the fore and aft fuselage 'box'. Wing contours were formed by numerous wooden ribs, which were covered by a plywood skin. The entire tail unit was spruce and plywood. As much of the airframe as possible was broken down into small wooden panels, which were ideal for sub-contracting to untapped sources of labour in an emergency, notably in the furniture manufacturing industry.

By June 1938 the Bristol and Armstrong Whitworth proposals had progressed to a point where design of the types could be studied in depth. On 15th of the month a design conference was held at Filton, Bristol, between the Bristol design team and representatives of the Air Ministry and Air Staff to assess the way Bristol had interpreted the B.9/38 specification and the potential of the resulting design. A similar conference was held a week later, on the 22nd, at Baginton, near Coventry, to discuss the Armstrong Whitworth B.9/38 design.

Following these conferences the Specification B.9/38 was discontinued, and two new specification numbers were allotted to the projects. In order to differentiate between the two, Specification B.17/38 was given to the Bristol design and B.18/38 to cover the Armstrong Whitworth project. Bristol gave the type number 155 to the B.17/38 and Armstrong Whitworth allotted the B.18/38 the type number AW 41.

The Bristol Aeroplane Company was heavily engaged in the development of the Blenheim and Beaufort, and towards the end of 1938 it started design of

the heavy fighter derivative of the Beaufort, powered by two Hercules engines. Development of this aircraft became a top-priority task for Bristol, and the decision was taken to discontinue further work on the B.17/38 bomber.

Armstrong Whitworth continued development of the B.18/38, which became finalised as a mid-wing bomber-reconnaissance aircraft with a wing span of 67ft and a length of 59ft 10½in. It was powered by two Bristol Hercules sleeve valve engines. Specification B.18/38 called for a speed, at economical cruising power, of not less than 250mph at 5,000ft. The aircraft had to be able to carry 1,500lb of bombs for 2,000 miles at 5,000ft.

An order for two prototypes (P1360 and P1361) and 298 production aircraft of the Armstrong Whitworth AW/41 was placed, under the type name Albemarle I,

The second prototype Albemarle, a P1361, on test in 1941.

production starting without waiting for prototype trials. Unlike other bomber types the Albermarle construction programme involved the placing of large numbers of small contracts with industries not usually associated with aircraft production, the parts being finally assembled for flight test at a new factory built for the purpose at Brockworth, Gloucester, known by the name of A. W. Hawksley Ltd (derived from Armstrong Whitworth and Hawker Siddeley). The first two prototypes were assembled by Air Service Training Ltd from sub-contracted parts. On the outbreak of war in September 1939 the original production order was increased to 1,000 Albemarles. It was intended that the aircraft would go into service with Bomber Command as a medium bomber and with Coastal Command in the general reconnaisance role alongside the Hudson.

The production of the aircraft proved to be more difficult than anticipated, owing to the complexity of the sub-contracted work, and there were long delays in obtaining components. The first prototype, P1360, was eventually completed early in 1940, and on March 20 that year it made its first flight when C. K. Turner-Hughes, Armstrong Whitworth's chief test pilot, found himself travelling too fast and rapidly running out of runway to stop in safety while conducting taxying tests at Hamble aerodrome. During previous taxying trials he had already noticed that the prototype showed little inclination to fly, and this unscheduled take-off, which was only achieved with the barest possible margin of safety, confirmed that the aircraft was deficient

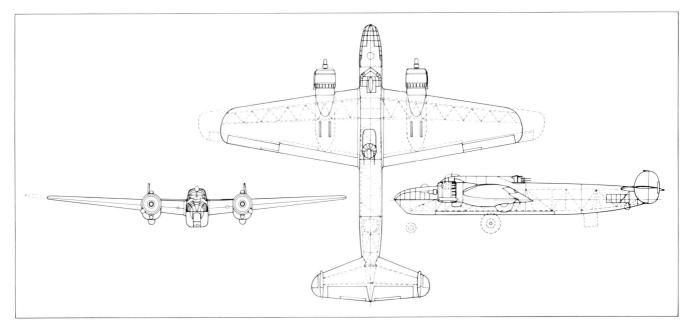

The first prototype of the Armstrong Whitworth Albemarle twin-engined composite-construction bomber. The drawing shows the aircraft in its original form with a wing span of 67ft. The wing extensions are shown dotted.

in wing area. It had been intended that the first 250 Albemarles would be completed as bombers, with subsequent aircraft being either for the bomber or general reconnaissance roles. The insufficient wing area meant an increase in wing span, which was incorporated into the·production line on the 9th production Albemarle. The take-off characteristics were so bad with the original wing that the loaded weight had to be restricted to 32,000lb instead of the initial clearance weight of 35,000lb on the first eight aircraft.

The new wing, with span increased to 77ft, was first test flown on the first production Albemarle, but further delay was caused to its introduction on the production line by the failure of Bomber Command to agree on what type of leading edge should be fitted.
5 Group favoured the use of balloon cable cutters, whereas 4 Group preferred to dispense with these in favour of de-icing equipment on the leading edge. Still more delay to the Albemarle programme was caused when the first prototype was damaged during a forced landing in September 1940 after a piece of wing skin had come adrift in the air.

By the end of 1940 it was becoming clear that the new bomber would not have sufficient advantage over existing twin-engined bombers to be acceptable to Bomber Command. Boscombe Down evaluated a production Albemarle, from which a complete assessment of the bomber's performance was ascertained. The weight of the bomber was 36,570lb and 70lb less for the reconnaissance version. Take-off in still air at 36,500lb required 1,240yd to clear 50ft. The top speed was around 245/250mph at 11,000/12,000ft and cruising speed for max. range was 170/180mph TAS. With the ventral turret down the speed was reduced by 10 per cent, with range reduced by 5 per cent. Time to reach 15,000ft was 30 minutes and the service ceiling was 17,500ft. 3,500lb of bombs could be carried for 1,300 miles (975 miles effective operational range), and

4,500lb of bombs for 1,050 miles (790 miles effective operational range). The reconnaissance mission could be flown for 2,060 miles (1,550 miles effective operational range).

The flying qualities of the Albemarle were very similar to those of the Wellington III. The controls were generally rather better than those of the Wellington, although the elevator was heavy. The view was good, except for straight ahead, when the aircraft had to be side-slipped or rocked sideways to view the runway. The tricycle undercarriage made landing easy. The crew layout was considered to be very good within the space limits, and the navigator's position was superior to that in any other contemporary aircraft.

The Albemarle, at the end of 1940, showed no advantage over the Wellington III from a performance standpoint, and was outclassed by the new production heavy bombers such as the Halifax, Stirling and Manchester. It was therefore decided not to use the Albemarle as a bomber. It had been intended to use the aircraft to supplement the Lockheed Hudson in Coastal Command, but the composite structure deteriorated rapidly in adverse weather conditions, with distortion of the plywood panelling. Aircraft on Coastal Command work faced unusually severe weather conditions when on patrol far out over the sea for long periods. The Albemarle was therefore also considered unsuitable for the second of the roles for which it was designed and it never entered service with Coastal Command. Eventually it was to fulfil a useful role as a transport and glider tug.

The Standard Bomber Project –B.1/39

Designs for a new four-engined bomber by Armstrong Whitworth, Avro, Blackburn, Bristol, etc.

With the B.12/36 and P.13/36 bomber designs well under development to meet Bomber Command's immediate requirements for bigger, harder-hitting bombers to replace the Whitley, Wellington and Hampden, the Air Staff turned their attention to the Command's longer term requirements.

It was evident from developments both in Britain and abroad, that future fighter aircraft would be primarily equipped with heavy-calibre weapons instead of rifle-calibre machine guns. It was true that British bomber defensive armament was, on many of the heavier types, more potent than any other used in the world at that time. The four-machine gun rear turret installed in such types as the Whitley, Stirling, Manchester and Halifax was a unique British development which gave these bombers formidable rear defence. The Air Staff, however, were of the opinion that the bomber carrying only .303 calibre guns would be at a grave disadvantage if attacked by enemy fighters equipped with heavy cannon.

The problem of installing heavy cannon for defence in bombers had already been investigated and conclusions drawn. The 20mm cannon was to be the new heavy calibre weapon for the RAF, but it was much larger than the existing Browning machine gun and its size made it unsuitable for installation in front and rear turrets. The resulting turret would have been so large as to cause unacceptable drag problems in a bomber of around 100ft span. It was thus felt that the only satisfactory positions for 20mm gun turrets would be in the mid-upper and mid-lower positions and that each turret should have the powerful punch of four 20mm cannon.

The previous year Boulton Paul and Frazer-Nash had developed designs for a circular, low profile, low-drag turret, armed with four 20mm guns, for the F.11/37 twin-engined fighter projects that they were developing. These turrets were to provide the basis for the B.1/39 bomber's defence. It was appreciated that the provision of such heavy armament would mean a reduction in bomb load of some 4,000lb, but this was considered to be justified.

The Air Staff formulated all their requirements for a future heavy bomber in Specification B.1/39, which was intended to evolve a potent long-range aircraft to ultimately replace all the RAF's existing types of medium and heavy bombers. The new bomber was required to carry a bomb load of 9,000lb over a range of at least 2,500 miles at a cruising speed, on maximum economical cruising power, of at least 280mph. The maximum bomb load was to be 10,000lb and part of it could be carried externally, if necessary, although the racks had to be dragless when bombs were not being carried. Like the B.12/36 and P.13/36 designs the B.1/39's bomb load was to comprise numbers of what in later years were to be considered as small bombs. Provision was to be made to stow the following loads: 20 x 500lb or 250lb bombs, 10 x 1,000lb bombs (then only in early production), 5 x 2,000lb armour-piercing bombs, 2 x 2,000lb SCI containers or 10 x small bomb containers. Without bomb load the B.1/39 was to be able to make ferry flights of 3,500 miles, possibly with the aid of auxiliary fuel tanks in the bomb bay.

The turrets, mounting four 20mm guns each, were to be designed so that their drag would only cause a 5 per cent decrease in the bomber's speed when compared with an unarmed version. They had to blend smoothly into the overall shape of the aircraft – as was also the case in respect of the F.11/37 project's turrets. Each of the 20mm guns was to be provided with five 30-round drums of ammunition, and an additional reserve supply of 20 drums of ammunition per turret was to be carried, but not necessarily inside the turrets. For certain missions, an additional 32 ammunition drums could be carried as an alternative to the bomb load. The aircraft was to be stressed to incorporate alternative turrets carrying two 40mm guns each with 110 rounds of ammunition if they became available and necessary.

The B.1/39 was required to maintain height with one engine out of action when carrying full bomb and fuel load in any weather and climatic conditions, at all altitudes up to 15,000ft. Take-off from a grass field in still air to clear a soft obstacle when carrying 9,000lb of bombs and fuel for 2,500 miles was to be made in not more than 900yd. Landing with full Service load for a range of 1,500 miles, but without bombs, was to be made in under 600yd after clearing a 50ft obstacle, under still air conditions.

Provision was to be made in the B.1/39 design for the aircraft to act as a troop carrier carrying 30 fully equipped men.

It was stipulated that in design of the structure the wing covering was not to be fabric. The restrictions on wing span imposed on the B.12/36 and P.13/36 designs were waived on the B.1/39 and designers were free to adopt any chosen layout to conform to the specification. It was also requested that aircraft designed to Specification B.1/39 should have four engines for reliability. The requirements of the specification and the lack of restrictions on wing span led to designers evolving aeroplanes of over 100ft span in all the designs tendered.

Preliminary instructions regarding the pending issue of Specification B.1/39 were sent to aircraft industry companies in a letter from the Directorate of Technical Development at the Air Ministry on January 5, 1939, and the specification was issued shortly afterwards. On January 26 a copy of the specification was sent to the RAE, Farnborough, for information and comment.

No less than nine firms submitted tenders to meet B.1/39 – Armstrong Whitworth, Avro, Blackburn, Bristol, Fairey, Gloster, Handley Page, Shorts and Vickers – which is hardly surprising when one remembers that the new bomber was intended to replace all existing medium and heavy bombers, and would therefore be needed in substantial numbers.

Shorts based their B.1/39 design tender on the Stirling, powered by either four Bristol Hercules HE7SM sleeve-valve radials or four Rolls-Royce Griffons conventionally mounted on the mid-wing. This was the only B.1/39 project with an orthodox undercarriage, all the others featuring the then-new tricycle layout. Shorts' tender, like everyone else's, dispensed with nose and tail turrets, but in its Hercules-powered form was the only one to have a single fin and rudder. The Griffon-powered version used twin fins and rudders.

Armstrong Whitworth's B.1/39 featured a very slim fuselage, with the wing merged by extensive fairings. This made turret fairing easier. Their design, powered by Rolls-Royce Griffons, was apparently to be constructed in composite materials like the Albemarle.

Gloster's B.1/39 also featured a slim fuselage, and the wing root matched it in depth, thus permitting the shallow, domed turrets to be merged into the upper and lower surfaces of the wing. The company preferred to use Bristol turrets, but Boulton Paul or Frazer-Nash turrets could be used as alternatives. Two different engine layouts were adopted, with preference for a four-Hercules installation. The alternative was for Hercules engines to be mounted on the outer nacelles and Bristol Centaurus engines mounted on the in-board nacelles. The tail unit featured twin fins and rudders.

Blackburn's project, too, adopted the principle of a thick wing centre section, extending to the full depth of the fuselage, in this case producing a wing root thickness/chord ratio of 30 per cent. Hercules or else Griffon engines were to power the aircraft and the turrets were to be of either Boulton Paul or Frazer-Nash design.

Avro based its B.1/39 on the Manchester, but with a four-engined layout – which may have helped to pave

The Armstrong Whitworth B.1/39 heavy bomber project. The aircraft is shown here with Rolls-Royce Griffons, but Bristol Hercules could be installed as alternatives. The project was apparently designed around a mixed wood and metal structure. The wing span was 104ft and the length was 85ft. A feature of the design was the use of a slim fuselage merged into a deep wing to facilitate the installation of the large-diameter low-profile turrets.

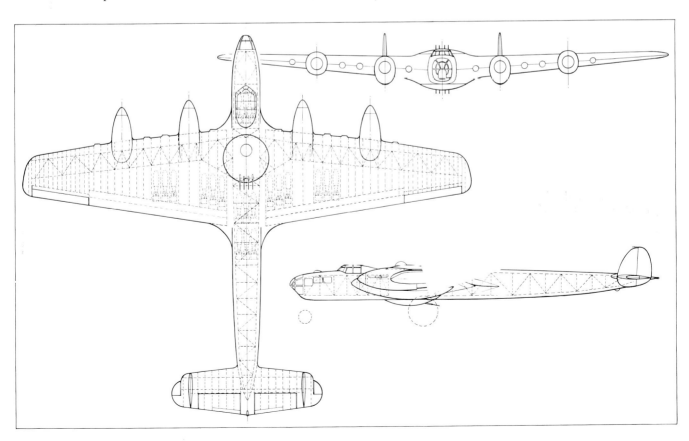

Main characteristics of B.1/39 designs

Range: 2,500 miles.

Company	Engines	Gross Weight (lb)	Struct Weight (lb)	Max Speed (mph)	Cruise Speed (mph)	Wing Span (ft)	Wing Area (sq ft)	Aspect Ratio	Wing Loading (lb/sq ft)
Armstrong Whitworth	Griffons	73,060	22,050	306	267	109	1,660	6.52	44.0
	Griffons	69,430	19,950	342	302	109	1,660	6.52	41.8
Blackburn	Hercules	72,233	20,447	296	272	104	1,814	5.95	39.8
Blackburn	Hercules	76,350	22,130	295	272	104	1,814	5.95	42.1
Blackburn	Griffons	73,167	20,575	302	265	104	1,814	5.95	40.9
Blackburn	Griffons	74,750	21,950	303	261	104	1,814	5.95	41.2
Bristol	Hercules	70,866	20,500	302	282	114	1,800	7.23	39.4
Bristol	Hercules	77,860	23,850	294	274	114	1,800	7.23	43.3
Bristol	Griffons	71,929	20,590	—	277	114	1,800	7.23	40.0
Bristol	Griffons	76,270	23,650	303	265	114	1,800	7.23	42.4
Fairey	Hercules	75,000	24,564	—	267	115	2,090	6.33	35.9
Fairey	Hercules	79,400	24,530	285	264	115	2,090	6.33	38.0
Fairey	P.24s	87,750	28,854	—	280	124	2,390	6.43	36.7
Fairey	P.24s	99,130	27,970	315	274	124	2,390	6.43	37.7
Gloster	Hercules	72,000	23,570	301	279	115	2,040	6.48	35.3
Gloster	Hercules	78,600	24,770	289	268	115	2,040	6.48	38.5
Handley Page	Hercules	71,000*	23,250	300	280	115	1,815	7.29	39.0
Handley Page	Hercules	77,090	23,850	295	273	115	1,815	7.29	42.3
Handley Page	Griffons	71,000*	23,510	315	277	115	1,815	7.29	39.0
Handley Page	Griffons	75,350	23,660	304	264	115	1,815	7.29	41.5
Avro	Hercules	72,230	23,080	324	271	120	1,835	7.85	39.4
Avro	Hercules	78,370	24,840	296	246	120	1,835	7.85	42.7
Short	Hercules	73,400	22,650	298	279	113.7	1,745	7.4	42.0
Short	Hercules	77,500	23,150	291	271	113.7	1,745	7.4	44.4
Short	Griffons	73,950	22,650	306	269	113.7	1,745	7.4	42.3
Short	Griffons	75,850	22,950	300	260	113.7	1,745	7.4	43.4
Vickers	Hercules	69,400	18,375	300	284	133	1,770	10	39.2
Vickers	Hercules	82,500	28,350	285	264	133	1,770	10	46.6
Vickers	Griffons	70,640	18,450	319	278	133	1,770	10	39.9
Vickers	Griffons	80,710	28,310	293	255	133	1,770	10	45.6

*Weight for 2,000 miles only.

the way for the eventual development of the Lancaster. Three different engine layouts were projected: four Bristol Hercules HE6SMs; four Rolls-Royce Griffons; or two Rolls-Royce Vultures and two Rolls-Royce Merlins. Avro favoured the use of Frazer-Nash turrets, with Boulton Paul as second choice. A tricycle undercarriage was adopted, and twin fins and rudders were used as on the Manchester.

Fairey also adopted a four-Hercules-powered project as first choice, with the engines mounted on a mid-wing, but an alternative design was drawn up using two of the big Fairey P.24 engines. These really consisted of two independent engines, coupled together through a common gearbox, driving a contra-prop. Each engine could be shut down, if desired, with its own propeller feathered, and thus the endurance of an aircraft could be greatly extended. The P.24-engined B.1/39 was similar in concept to the Heinkel He 177, although in the latter case the coupled engines could not be shut down independently.

Vickers adopted a mid-wing, twin-tail, tricycle undercarriage, layout for their B.1/39. The wing had a graceful elliptical plan-form with four nacelles housing either Bristol Hercules or Rolls-Royce Griffon engines. Turrets were to be of Frazer-Nash design, rotating through 360 degrees with minimal blind spots. An unusual feature of the design was the provision of four main undercarriage units, one retracting into each nacelle. This was a further development of the layout used for the company's unsuccessful B.12/36 tender.

The Vickers design was understandably based on the geodetic construction which had proved so successful in the Wellington. Owing to the requirement laid down in the specification regarding wing covering, a special skin of bonded Alclad (thin aluminium sheet) and very thin plywood was developed for this purpose. The Alclad and plywood skins were bonded together with synthetic rubber, the plywood being so thin that it would become impregnated with the bonding rubber. The fuselage, tailplane and fins and rudders, as well as the ailerons and elevators, were all to be fabric-covered. Vickers were convinced that experience in all climates with fabric covering, including the extensive use of Wellesleys in the Middle East, showed that it was quite satisfactory as a wing covering. They felt that the Air Ministry should consider waiving the ruling about using a non-fabric wing covering on the B.1/39 as this would make possible a weight saving of 470lb on their particular project and also reduce production man-hours

The Griffon-powered Vickers B.1/39 project had an estimated top speed of 332mph compared with the top speed of 312mph of the Hercules-powered version, but the Hercules-powered aircraft cruised at the higher speed of 284mph instead of 278mph attained with four Griffons.

Vickers prepared an alternative B.1/39 tender emplying conventional all-metal, stressed-skin construction, but in order to obtain the same take-off and landing performance they had to increase the wing area and consequently the span – from 133ft to 143ft. This, in turn, led to the adoption of a larger tail unit, with the final result that the estimated structure weight

The Vickers-Armstrongs B.1/39 geodetic heavy bomber. The wing structure, built around a geodetic box spar, was intended to be covered by a thin metal sheet and plywood sandwich skin. The fuselage and tail unit were intended to be covered by fabric. Alternate sandwich skins were designed for the fuselage and tail unit, although these would have been heavier. An alternate stressed-skin metal structure was also designed for the project if this was required instead of the geodetic structure. The elliptical wing, four-main undercarriage layout was revived from the Vickers B.12/36 project and was later used on the Vickers Windsor heavy bomber.

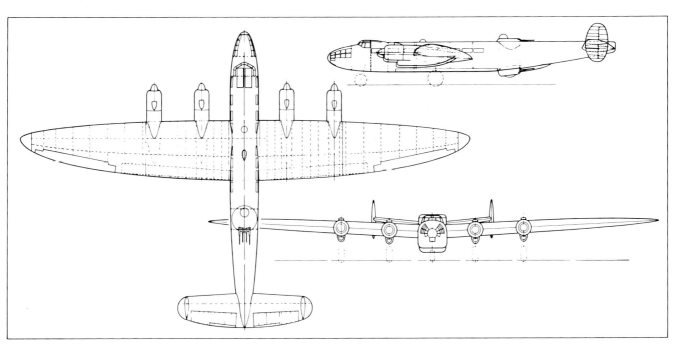

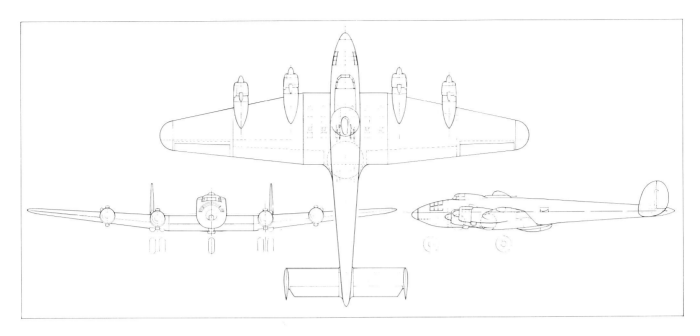

went up by 5,000lb while the estimated cruising speed was reduced by 7mph.

Handley Page developed their B.1/39 from the Halifax, but it was unique among the B.1/39 designs in having a high-wing configuration. This arrangement eased the problem of merging the 14ft diameter upper turret into the fuselage 'wing structure' to achieve smooth, low-drag contours. The high-wing layout, of course, necessitated the use of a long undercarriage, again of tricycle form with the mainwheel units retracting sideways into the wing. The tail unit incorporated twin fins and rudders. Powerplant was four Bristol Hercules HE7SM radials or four Rolls-Royce Griffons, and the turrets were to be of Boulton Paul or Frazer-Nash design.

The Bristol tender was also unique among the B.1/39 projects in featuring a low-set wing design, with emphasis on merging the large-diameter ventral turret into the wing/fuselage contours. Bristol turrets were designed for this project, with Frazer-Nash as alternatives, and the dorsal turret was smaller and more compact than the low profile ventral turret. As on other B.1/39 designs the navigator's compartment was in the extreme nose. The undercarriage was of tricycle type. Designated the Bristol Type 159, the bomber was powered by four Bristol Hercules HE7SM engines as first choice, with Rolls-Royce Griffons as alternatives. At the time the Bristol project was the largest and heaviest aircraft ever designed by the company.

From the many B.1/39 design tenders the Air Ministry selected two, those of Handley Page and Bristol, for prototype development and production; contracts for the prototypes were duly placed. Handley Page apparently intended to build a half-scale model of their B.1/39 design before full scale construction commenced. Bristols started cutting metal for test sections of theirs. Eventually, development of the all-purpose heavy bomber to replace all existing types was abandoned in favour of increased production of existing types, and the orders for prototypes were cancelled.

The Bristol B.1/39 heavy bomber design, which was ordered for prototype development and on which construction was begun. This promising and advanced design was cancelled in 1940, probably to permit Bristols to concentrate on Beaufighter development and because in general the B.1/39s did not comply with new policies regarding the carriage of smaller numbers of very large high-capacity bombs. As in many of the B.1/39 designs, the Bristol bomber carried much of the bomb load in wing cells, to allow the heavy turrets to be mounted near to the CG. Even if not required as a bomber, it is surprising that the aircraft was not developed for the long-range maritime recce. role, for which it seemed well-suited. The wing span was 114ft. Six 2,000lb AP bombs are shown in the wing cells.

Advent of the High Speed Unarmed Bomber

The de Havilland Mosquito.

During 1935 the Royal Aircraft Establishment at Farnborough undertook a series of hypothetical design studies of high speed twin-engined medium bombers for the Directorate of Technical Development. These designs were investigated to give the DTD information on possible future trends in bomber design, which would assist in formulating new specifications.

Two of these designs considered what performance would result from the installation of two Rolls-Royce Merlin engines of 1,000hp each in a bomber of approx

60ft span and a length of 37.5ft – one with gun turret armament for defence and the other a smooth unarmed aircraft relying on speed for defence. It was considered that, at an all-up weight of 18,000lb, it would be possible to achieve a speed of 329mph in the case of the latter design, while the addition of turret armament would reduce the speed by 14mph. It was considered that the unarmed bomber would be able to fly for 1,320 miles when carrying a bomb load of 1,750lb. To produce a really smooth, contoured aeroplane a method of skin evaporative cooling could be employed, but if this was not acceptable low drag could be achieved by installing wing radiators.

This design study for an unarmed, twin-Merlin bomber is remarkably close to the eventual Mosquito design in concept, and when allowance is made for the smaller size, lower weight, smaller bomb load and higher power of the de Havilland bomber, it can be seen that the performance estimated was also quite realistic for the technology of 1935.

It is not known if de Havilland's chief engineer, C. C. Walker, had access to the RAE's work on theoretical bomber design, but such information was often made available to the aircraft industry and it is probable

that it was made available to de Havillands. Captain Geoffrey de Havilland and Walker were in close contact with the Air Council Member for Research and Development, Sir Wilfred Freeman, who must have been familiar with the RAE's work and may well have brought it to the attention of de Havillands.

In May 1937 the de Havilland Albatross airliner made its first flight, an aircraft of very advanced design and surely one of the most elegant and beautiful aeroplanes of all time. Like the company's special Comet racing aircraft, the Albatross was of wood construction, which resulted in an extremely smooth exterior finish. Powered by four de Havilland Gipsy Twelve Srs I engines of 525hp each, the Albatross could carry a 6,000lb payload over a range that would include Berlin and back, cruising at 210mph. With such a performance a military version of the aircraft seemed to have possibilities and a project was drafted which would conform to Specification P.13/36. This was projected with two Rolls-Royce Merlin engines, but this bomber was underpowered and not able to meet the specification requirement. With Merlins the top speed would have been 260mph and it could carry 4,000lb of bombs at 230mph for 1,500 miles. To meet the specification,

double the power was needed, which was not surprising as all the other P.13/36 designs projected were mostly using two Vultures, with Sabres, Centaurus or Hercules as alternative power plants.

In August 1938 a revised twin-Merlin bomber was projected – again of similar size to the Albatross – but it too proved unsatisfactory.

Towards the end of 1938 de Havilland proposed a different bomber layout, no longer an adaptation of the Albatross design but a smaller, three-seat twin-Merlin design with a top speed of 300mph and a cruising speed of 268mph. This design had fixed forward armament and manually-operated guns. All-wood construction was again suggested.

This proposal was put forward around the time of the Munich crisis. Europe seemed to be moving closer to war, and the aircraft industry was generally very busy with large production orders and development contracts. de Havillands had built up a thriving company on civil aircraft designs and had little experience of

The prototype Mosquito, with original Class B registration, is prepared for engine runs at Hatfield in November 1940.

designing aeroplanes to Air Ministry specifications. As war seemed to be inevitable at some time in the near future, de Havillands were anxious to obtain government contracts to replace the civil market which would soon diminish. They were also anxious to keep together their design organisation which would become redundant if the company became merely sub-contractors to other companies. The future prosperity of the company depended on the acceptance of a home-designed product for development.

Another project was considered: a bomber variant of the DH95 Flamingo airliner, which had been designed as an all-metal aircraft able to carry 12-20 passengers. The bomber variant could carry a 2,000lb bomb load, and could fly for 1,500 miles. This project was considered towards the end of 1938, but it offered little advantage over existing bomber designs and was not as advanced as some under development.

During the last months of peace during 1939 de Havillands investigated various projects, during the course of which they held discussions with Sir Wilfred Freeman. From these discussions it seems probable that the first definite proposals for a fast, small, unarmed bomber made of wood was evolved. By September 1939 the de Havilland project team had finalised a design for a fast bomber with a crew of two, powered by two Rolls-Royce engines using 100 octane fuel. This unarmed aircraft was estimated to carry two 500lb or six 250lb bombs for 1,500 miles cruising at 320mph. Top speed was 405mph.

In a letter to Sir Wilfred Freeman written on September 20, Capt de Havilland wrote, 'We have stopped all civil design and want to put our whole design staff on to war work. From former conversations with you, and using the experience we have gained in very quickly producing types which have to compete with others from all over the world, we believe that we could produce a twin-engined bomber which would have a performance so outstanding that little defensive equipment would be needed. This would employ the well tried out methods of design and construction used in the Comet and the Albatross and, being of wood or composite construction, would not encroach on the labour and material used in expanding the RAF. It is specially suited to really high speeds because all surfaces are smooth, free from rivets, overlapped plates and undulations. It also lends itself to very rapid initial and subsequent production . . .'

In a postscript to this letter Capt de Havilland stated, 'I am anxious to get this preliminary proposal in to you without delay, but will just add that it has been based on the availability of Merlin engines. Were it possible to use Sabres the same performance and range could be obtained with 4,000lb of bombs, crew of three and two guns.'

The new de Havilland aircraft was given the company designation DH98 and the preliminary proposal for this twin-Merlin design was examined by members of the Air Staff and Air Ministry. The idea of a completely unarmed bomber aircraft, relying entirely on speed for defence, aroused some scepticism. During the first few months of the war the Bristol Blenheim had been very successful in evading enemy defences because of its fairly high speed. Its loss rate had been about one aircraft per fifteen sorties, but the RAF was of the opinion that this was more due to lack of experience and organisation of the enemy defences rather than the Blenheim's performance, which was insufficiently high to be immune from fighter interception. This opinion was to be confirmed later during the Battle of France. There was some doubt whether the DH98, operating in the conventional bomber role, would be able to remain ahead of enemy fighter speed performance. With an estimated top speed of 405mph, there were fears, not unjustified, that the DH98 would not be fast enough. At this time there were a number of British fighters under active development with speeds of well over 400mph and it was expected that Germany would produce fighters of similar performance. It was also true that the majority of aircraft suffered a reduction in performance due to normal wear and tear under service conditions, and due to the inevitable weight increases brought about by modifications and additional equipment. The Air Staff were of the opinion that some form of simple rear defence should be built into the design, similar to the twin-gun emplacement used on the Hampden, if only to act as scare weapons to put an enemy fighter off its aim while the bomber pilot sought the sanctuary of cloud cover. de Havillands considered this problem and its effect on performance. In a letter to the Deputy Director of Research and Development at the Air Ministry, H. Grinstead, de Havilland chief engineer C. C. Walker stated '. . . As you say the Production Branch is now considering this project I must give you some further information concerning it. The scheme has now undergone some evolution as a result of what we have been able to hear about war experience up to now coupled with what you have told us of the Air Ministry's views about rear defence for bombers.

'The scheme mentioned in my letter of 19th October envisaged the use of Merlin engines and a fairly simple rear gun emplacement for two guns with a reasonably good cone of fire. This arrangement as I pointed out would cost from 20 to 30mph in max. speed.

'We now think it would be best to retain the high speed and make the rear defence first class by using a full four gun turret and achieve these objects by using the Griffon engine. We should like to have the opportunity of going more closely into the speed of this machine, but can give it approximately now as from 390 to 400mph at 20,000ft. The size of machine is increased from our original proposal to retain a wing-loading of just over 30lb per sq ft for landing.

'If the Griffon engine machine were looked on as the basic type, it would also take Merlins with the simpler gun emplacement already described without any undue difficulties about change of trim, etc.

'The basic type would then have the following main characteristics:

Two Griffon engines.
Max speeds 390 to 400mph at 20,000ft.
1,000lb bombs (2 x 500lb GP or gas or armour piercing.
Or 6 x 250lb. Also provision for 4 small bomb containers).
Space for 1,500lb bombs.
1,500 miles range with 2,000 miles for overload case.
4 gun turret in tail (Frazer-Nash armoured).
Crew of three. Armour behind pilot.
. . .'

This letter went on to mention the advantage of using wooden construction in the project and the use of labour and materials that did not encroach upon other programmes. It was suggested that if an order was placed quickly the type could be delivered in numbers in 18 months from the receipt of an order. de Havillands wanted a small batch of aircraft to be ordered because they could not put all their design effort into producing just one prototype.

The problem of rear defence caused a lot of discussion at the Air Ministry. The RAF was not opposed to the idea of an unarmed aircraft operating over Germany, provided that it was not used against alerted defences. It was felt that such an aircraft would suit the reconnaissance role. The RAF considered the main bombing type to be the long range, very large, well-armed heavy bomber, but there was also a need for a smaller, faster bomber that could make a second strike against a target bombed a few hours earlier – one that could penetrate well-alerted defences. The RAF had asked for a high-speed bomber for such tasks, but opinions on the form this should take were divided. The DH98 was but one proposal being considered among a number of different schemes.

In order to discuss plans for a high-speed bomber, and to examine the de Havilland proposals a conference was held at King Charles Street, Whitehall, on December 12, 1939, with the Acting Chief of the Air Staff in the chair. Among those present were the Air Member for Development and Production, the Director General of Research and Development, the Commander-in-Chief Bomber Command, the Director General of Operations, and the Director of Operational Requirements. This conference was one of the most significant held, and from it stemmed two major decisions which were to have far-reaching consequences for Bomber Command.

The Acting Chief of the Air Staff outlined the reason for convening the conference, which was to consider further the various forms of high speed bomber that had been put forward by the C-in-C Bomber Command. The conclusion had been reached that to try and combine exceptionally high speed with modern armament and other requirements would result in a bad compromise aircraft.

The Air Member for Development and Production said that speed versus armament was the crux of the matter. What speed was required in relation to contemporary fighters? If an aircraft were to be produced which would carry a small bomb load and be faster than contemporary fighters, would Bomber Command be prepared to dispense with all defensive armament?

The C-in-C Bomber Command said that such an aircraft would not meet the particular requirements, but there would always be a use for such an aircraft for reconnaissance duties. His requirement was for an aircraft to take over the duties performed by the Blenheim, which were to penetrate over enemy country singly or in small formations, reconnoitre, take photographs, carry out bombing attacks and stand a good chance of evading interception. At the beginning of the war the Blenheim had been fast enough to avoid interception except for about one in 15 sorties, but this ratio was now rapidly diminishing and a faster aircraft was now needed. An aircraft was required that would be able to follow up the destructive work of the heavy bombers by harassing the enemy and interfering with attempts to repair damage and deal with fires. Such a bomber would be liable to interception by fighters expecting further attacks, and would need to defend itself. Such an aircraft would therefore need good facilities for navigation and bomb aiming, sufficient armour, self-sealing tanks and sufficient defensive armament to give the crew confidence that they had a fighting chance. The requirements for this aircraft were different from those for a high-speed reconnaissance aircraft (in the latter case, these aircraft operated often singly and the enemy had little warning of such a mission, and was less prepared for interception).

The AMDP thought it would be necessary to have two distinct types, a high speed recce aircraft and an unarmed, high speed bomber. It was accepted in the case of the latter aircraft that a new version would come out each year with increased engine power that would maintain an ascendancy in speed over the contemporary fighter.

From statements made during this conference it is obvious that the requirement for a fast reconnaissance aircraft was being met by a small order for a special version of the Westland Whirlwind, which was not armed except for a small bomb load.

Bomber Command still wanted a fast bomber which could carry a small bomb load, have armour and self-sealing tanks, a good view to rearward and some form of armament. The Acting Chief of the Air Staff pointed out that a Bristol Beaufort with Hercules engines would have a top speed of 320mph, and it was doubtful, unless adequate time was given for development, whether any new design would have much advantage over this.

It was discussed whether or not Bomber Command's requirements might not be met from types already in production or under development. It was considered that the Manchester could be made faster and im-improved by installing more powerful engines, and generally cleaning up the design, but that such a development would take rather more than two years. It was suggested that there could be a danger of dis-locating existing production by making demands on skilled labour. There could be an advantage in using wooden construction, and having the project produced by a firm like de Havillands. The C-in-C Bomber Command, whilst pressing for a new high-speed bomb-er, urgently, also thought that a long-term project such as that suggested for development of the Manchester should be pursued concurrently.

After detailed examination of the scheme put for-ward by de Havillands, from whom it was hoped to have deliveries in nine months, it was agreed that two schemes should be pursued. Scheme I was for an air-craft of wooden construction on the lines of the DH98. The aircraft would have a crew of two, be unarmed, would carry a 1,000lb bomb load, and have a range of 1,500 miles. It would have self-sealing tanks and would carry a camera. The re-engining of this aircraft as necessary to keep pace with contemporary fighter development would be borne in mind. Scheme II would be for a very high speed, large bomber based on the Manchester.

In the interim the Air Staff were asked to consider the possibility of providing Bomber Command with two squadrons of Beauforts, possibly cleaned up in the manner undertaken on the Blenheim. (Experiments into cleaning up the Blenheim to get higher speed had been undertaken by Wing Commander Cotton's Flight at Heston, which was the unit from which PRU was evolved. The measures taken to increase Blenheim

speed included sealing badly fitting doors and panels, filling skin joints and the introduction of the Type S surface finish system, which produced a smoother external finish. New camouflage paints were introduced with the Type S system, of much more refined, smoother texture. This replaced the old matt Type M finish on Blenheims.)

The conference held at Whitehall on December 12, 1939, was responsible for two important decisions: a small order for the DH98 was sanctioned, and develop-ment of a new bomber based on the Manchester was ordered, which led to the Lancaster.

As a result of the acceptance of de Havillands' proposals, an order for 50 was authorised under the specification number 1/40, which laid down per-formance requirements. It was decided that the air-craft should be fitted with two Rolls-Royce Merlin RM2SM engines. It was suggested that no separate order for prototypes would be given, but the first six aircraft would be considered as prototypes. It was also borne in mind that if the project was successful further follow-up orders would be given, if necessary with up-rated engines. The specification called for an unarmed reconnaissance bomber with a crew of two in a heated and armoured cockpit, a 1,000lb bomb load and a range of 1,500 miles. Self-sealing tanks, W/T equip-

The Armstrong Whitworth B.7/40 twin-engined light bomber. The B.7/40 requirement was intended to be a Blenheim replacement, but was not ordered. This twin-Merlin project was, like the Albemarle and Armstrong Whitworth B.1/39, a typical product of John Lloyd's design team during the immediate pre-war and early war era. The AW B.7/40 had a wing span of 54ft and a length of 46ft, making it similar in size to the Mosquito. It carried a bomb load of 1,000lb and was armed with four fixed Browning guns firing forward and two similar .303in guns in the tail turret. The design was stressed for dive bombing and had dive brakes under the wings. It carried a crew of four.

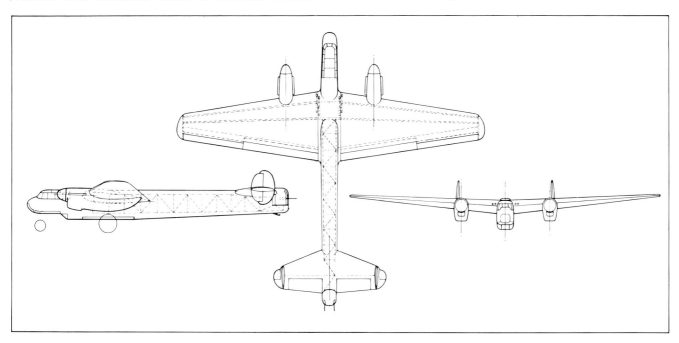

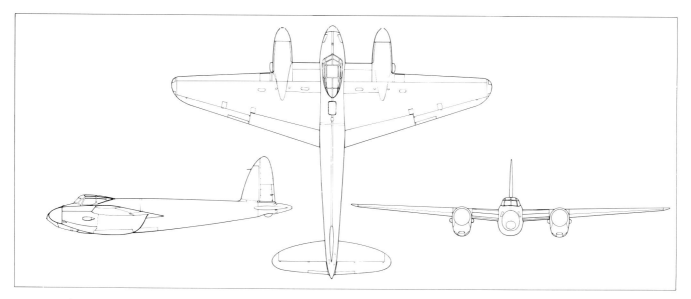

ment and a camera would be carried. It was expected that the first aircraft would be flying within nine months of the order to proceed being given. Later the DH98 was given the name by which it was to become a household word – Mosquito.

The discussions at the conference also led to another requirement, that of the slower, armed bomber to replace the Blenheim, which was embodied in Specification B.7/40.

It is also possible that the decision to develop a new bomber from the Manchester may have caused the B.1/39 requirement to be re-assessed and eventually abandoned when the decision was taken to concentrate on a few basic types already in production.

The formal contract for the initial batch of Mosquitoes was placed with de Havillands on March 1, 1940, by which time detailed design work was well advanced. The estimated cost of each Mosquito was £14,200, a total cost of £710,000 for the 50 aircraft. These aircraft were to conform of Specification B.1/40, which was drawn up around the Mosquito project.

The batch of 50 Mosquitoes commenced with W4050, which was regarded as the aerodynamic prototype. The second aircraft, W4051, was to act as the test aircraft for the operational bomber-reconnaissance role. The third, W4052, was to be produced as a two-seat fighter, a role always borne in mind for the aircraft.

As finalised, the Mosquito was an exceedingly 'clean' and beautiful aircraft, with a wing span of 52ft 6in. The two Rolls-Royce Merlin RM3SM engines were mounted in nacelles which terminated under the wing immediately forward of the flaps. The crew of two were housed under a canopy of very smooth form. In the extreme nose was a glazed section, with an optically flat window for accurate bomb aiming. The 'cleanliness' of the engine nacelles was enhanced by the installation of the radiators in the leading edge of the inner wing.

Construction of the Mosquito was all wood, develop-

The de Havilland Mosquito 1st prototype, W4050 or originally E0234, as it appeared during early flight trials in late November, 1940. W4050 had a wing span of 52ft 6in, but on production aircraft this was increased to 54ft 2in. W4050 had a tailplane span of 19ft 6in, but this too was increased on later aircraft to 20ft 9in. With Rolls-Royce Merlin RM3SM engines W4050 had a top speed of 392mph at 22,000ft.

ed from the Albatross. The fuselage was built in two halves split directly down the entire length, and joined after the addition of equipment, pipe runs and control cables. Assembly was as in a present day plastic construction kit. Thick, stressed skins were used, consisting of a sandwich of thin birch plywood outer panels, with a balsa wood centre filling. Spruce was used for heavy spars, frames and webs, often with birch ply covering. The wing skins were birch ply with fifteen supporting spanwise stringers. Fuel tank·panels, situated on the wing underside, were constructed of birch ply and balsa sandwich. Extreme surface smoothness was obtained by covering the wood exterior with fabric.

The Mosquito was expected to reach a speed of 397mph at 23,700ft. Cruising speed was expected to be 327mph at 26,600ft. Range was estimated as 1,480 miles at 343mph at 24,900ft. Estimated weights were 18,845lb max for the bomber version and 17,150lb for a normally-loaded PR aircraft.

Work on the first prototype continued at a high rate during the early part of 1940, but in May, when France and the Low Countries were invaded on the 10th, the war began in earnest on the Continent opposite Britain. Lord Beaverbrook had taken over the new Ministry of Aircraft Production and plans were drawn up to concentrate production on a few selected types. The types selected were those well-established in production, newer types being given second priority. The Mosquito was then regarded as a very new experimental aircraft of unknown potential. It could prove to be outstanding, or prove to be totally incorrect in conception if the enemy had fighter aircraft able to intercept it on

operations. It was therefore not included on the list of priority aircraft and briefly work stopped on the new bomber.

Because it made little call on usual aircraft materials it was reinstated on the second priority list on July 12. Work resumed on the prototype throughout the difficult days of the summer of 1940, with interruptions caused by the many air raid alerts. Further set-backs occurred on October 3 when a Ju88 inadvertently found Hatfield, in the poor visibility, instead of its primary target of Reading. Before being shot down it dropped four 250kg bombs on the de Havilland works, destroying materials and work in progress for the Mosquito. Fortunately, the prototype was being constructed at Salisbury Hall a few miles from Hatfield and was not directly affected.

On November 3, 1940, the completed components of the first prototype – which, for convenience, will henceforth be referred to merely as 'the prototype', were transferred from Salisbury Hall to Hatfield for assembly and preparation for flight trials. By the middle of November the aircraft was complete and ready for engine runs. It was painted overall in yellow to give it the outward appearance of a trainer aircraft, and at this stage carried the Class B serial EO234.

On November 24 the prototype, with the chief test pilot, Geoffrey de Havilland junior, at the controls and John E. Walker, DH engine installation designer in the right-hand seat, was taxied out for its first tests. The time was 1500hr and a 5mph south-west wind was gently blowing across the field. The intention on this test of the aircraft under free power for the first time was to check taxiing behaviour at both low and high speeds. It was not intended to fly the aircraft on this occasion. The Mosquito weighed 14,150lb. During ordinary taxiing, the aircraft showed a tendency to swing, which was thought at the time to be due either to an idling speed that was too high on the port engine (750rpm on port, 450rpm on starboard), or to a binding brake. The true cause was later traced to the tailwheel, which was not castoring correctly.

Several short take-off runs were commenced, opening up the engines to +11lb boost for a moment. The Mosquito showed the great powers of acceleration obtainable and the tail came up readily. Runs were made with up to 10 per cent of flap. The aerodrome surface was slippery and the brakes tended to lock. On its last run of the day the aircraft became airborne for a brief moment. It is interesting to note in this day of computerised flight test data recording that it was not possible to record the speed at which the Mosquito became airborne due to the need to observe the heavy traffic on the aerodrome! The test ended at 1530hr. All was now set to take the new bomber into its true element.

November 25 again found a gentle 5mph breeze blowing from the south-west, and at 1545hr Geoffrey de Havilland Jnr and John Walker taxied out the Mosquito for that big moment in any new aeroplane's life. The aircraft again weighed 14,150lb.

There was some concern about the possibility of the flaps moving independently from their settings. The two large flaps were linked mechanically through a series of links but it was considered possible that there could be sufficient play in the mechanism to produce unequal settings, with disastrous results. To check this, the first test of the day was to be a short hop, in which the Mosquito would be taken off briefly, the power cut and the aircraft landed immediately. The flap take-off setting of 15 degrees would then be checked to ensure that movement had not taken place. Geoffrey de Havilland Jnr and John Walker carried out this test and the aircraft was then taxied back for the check to be made. The check showed both flaps at exactly 15 degrees. All was well, and now the real work of the day would be carried out.

This time on its take-off run the aircraft was lifted from the aerodrome in a straightforward and easy manner and continued to climb up to considerable height before undercarriage retraction was carried out, which was observed by John Walker through the bomb aimer's window. It was noticed that the main undercarriage doors remained open, about 4 inches width between the doors remaining at the speed at which the Mosquito flew. As speed was increased, so the doors opened increasingly – the gap increasing to 12 inches at higher speeds. The speed at this gap width was 220mph IAS, the highest attained on this first flight. Little change of trim was noticed during retraction of the wheels.

At a good height for safety the undercarriage was lowered and the flaps were depressed to 25 degrees to test the aircraft's behaviour near the stall – so that there would not be any surprises during the landing approach and touch-down. Aileron control remained good and the Mosquito showed promise at low speed of being a tractable aircraft. The new bomber-reconnaissance aircraft was afterwards brought in for its first landing, at a speed of approx 120mph. Even though the Mosquito had been held off rather too high there was no sign of lateral instability and the aircraft touched the ground with the minimum of shock. It had been a successful first flight. The door opening problem would be solved, but it was to take quite a time before a real cure was found.

After this flight the aircraft was taken back to the flight test hangar for examination and attempts to find out the cause of the door problem.

On November 29 the prototype with Geoffrey de Havilland Jnr and John Walker in the cabin, took off for its second flight. This time a 13mph wind was blowing from the west. The all-up weight on this flight was 15,187lb and this test took 20 minutes. The third flight, also on this day, was of 35 minutes' duration. R. E. Bishop, head of the Mosquito design team, was

Geoffrey de Havilland's companion on this flight. On these flights stalling was carried out, with 50 degrees of flap. Only slight starboard wing dropping occurred at the stall. Lateral and directional stability of the Mosquito was also checked, which seemed to be good. The problem with the main undercarriage doors opening increasingly with speed remained unsolved.

On December 5 three more flights were carried out, totalling 1hr 15min. Geoffrey de Havilland Jnr was again the pilot, but his observers on these flights were Mr Bishop, Mr Clarkson and his father, Capt Geoffrey de Havilland. General test flying was carried out. The door problem persisted and tailwheel castoring trouble was again encountered. A significant problem was met on the first flight of the day when tail buffet was felt at 240-250mph IAS. This, together with the doors being continually forced open, led to suspicions that the airflow around the nacelles was not all that it should be, and it was therefore decided to wool tuft the nacelles. After completing these flights the total Mosquito time in the air was 2hr 30min. The wind speed of the aerodrome on this day was 15mph but the wind from the south-west was increasing.

The next day a 60mph gale was blowing across Hatfield, but the Mosquito prototype was again brought out from the hangar for test flying. The weight of the aircraft was again 15,187lb and the pilot was Geoffrey de Havilland Jnr, who was accompanied on this flight by B. Cross, as test observer. This test was to check single-engined handling, but after a 15min flight the test was abandoned owing to oil pressure failure. During landing the Mosquito behaved in a very reassuring manner in the gusty 60mph wind.

After correction to the oil pressure two further flights were made on December 6. During one of these flights Bishop and Clarkson were housed in the rear fuselage, primarily to observe the behaviour of the wool tufts that were now attached all over the aft part of the nacelles, but also to retract the tailwheel which was not at this time integral with the main hydraulic circuit. Wool tufts on the outer part of the nacelles could be observed from another aircraft in the air, but inner nacelle airflow could only be seen from the rear fuselage. It was obvious from the disturbed airflow patterns observed that turbulence had been responsible for tail vibration felt above 240mph IAS.

On the second of these flights, made with the ground speed reduced to 20mph, the first single-engined test was carried out. The Mosquito behaved well, no vicious tendencies being observed.

To try to correct the nacelle airflow problem special airflow correction slats were fitted around the rear of the nacelle and under the inner wing. These acted in a similar manner to present day vortex generators. This solution was not successful, success ultimately coming from lengthening the rear of the nacelles.

By December 11 the Mosquito prototype had made 30 flights.

High-altitude Bombers

Development of the Vickers Wellington V.

Development work at the Royal Aircraft Establishment, Farnborough, on the design of pressure cabins, the flying of a specially adapted pressure cabin-equipped version of the General Aircraft Monospar, the encouraging development at Bristol of the high-altitude version of the Hercules engine and similar work on the Merlin engine at Derby, convinced the Air Ministry that it would be feasible to produce a range of bombers capable of operating at extreme altitudes. The Air Staff were sure that, given special bomb sights of great accuracy, a bomber could attack targets from above 35,000ft, where it would be almost immune from fighters.

Further assessment of high-altitude bombers led to the issue of Specification B.35/37 for the design of two bombers, one to operate at 25,000ft and the other above 40,000ft. Both types were to have a pressure cabin and were to be four-engined. It was suggested that the power plant should be the high-altitude Merlin with two-stage superchargers and that the aircraft should also have a tricycle undercarriage. The aircraft were to be armed with 20mm cannon, with four firing to the rear and beamwards, and two more firing forward. It was proposed that the '25,000ft' aeroplane should be developed from the Stirling and the '40,000ft' type from one of the P.13/36 bombers – preferably the Halifax.

Although project work was done on these aeroplanes, they were not developed – probably because both the B.12/36 and P.13/36 bombers' wings were of low aspect ratio, due to the span restriction of up to 100ft, and thus unsuitable for high-altitude aircraft. The Stirling, in particular, was already handicapped as regards altitude performance at full load.

Adaptation of another well-tried design to the high-altitude bomber role met with more success. In the autumn of 1938 Vickers were asked to investigate the design of a high-altitude version of the Wellington, operating normally at 35,000ft with a maximum ceiling of 40,000ft. The aircraft was to have a cylindrical pressure cabin, which would house the entire crew during operations at very high altitudes. To cover this development, Specification B.23/39 was issued. At maximum height the cabin pressure was to remain at an equivalent altitude of 10,000ft, a cabin pressure of 7lb/sq in. Vickers had not experienced such a requirement before, but their pressure cabin design was very successful and the adaptation of the basic Wellington fuselage to-mount the long cylinder proved to be relatively easy. No armament was fitted in the nose of the aircraft, but a four .303in gun turret was installed in the tail, operated remotely from the cabin.

Two prototypes of the high-altitude Wellington were ordered under the designation Mk V and they were to be powered by two Bristol Hercules VIII engines with exhaust-driven superchargers. Owing to delays in engine development, the first prototype, R3298, was fitted with Hercules IIIs and it was first flown in early September 1940. The second prototype, R3299, flew in November 1940, powered by Hercules VIIIs.

Flying trials revealed that the power output of the Hercules was below expectation, and the required ceiling was not attained. Thus, although a production order for 30 Wellington Vs had been placed, only nine were eventually completed and they never saw squadron service. Nevertheless, the type did provide Vickers with valuable experience in designing and operating pressure cabins and provided the basis for, among other things, the similarly-configured Wellington VI of 1941, which was powered by Merlin 60 engines.

Above: The first prototype Wellington V, R3298, takes-off in late 1940 from Vickers' wartime airfield at Squires Gate, Blackpool, where it had been based for trials following enemy air attacks on Vickers' Weybridge facility.

Top right: The boiler-like pressure cabin in the nose of the Wellington V before being completely faired in.

Above right: In this side view of the first prototype Wellington V the type's ungainly lines are seen to advantage.

Below: The second prototype Wellington V, R3299. Compare the cockpit transparency with that of R3298.

Operations: The 'Phoney War'

At the outbreak of World War II, on September 3, 1939, Bomber Command was 55 squadrons strong, but on the previous day the 10 Fairey Battle squadrons which formed 1 Group flew to France as the 1st Echelon of the Advanced Air Striking Force – which latter was, in effect, an extension of Bomber Command, and a force whose story will be dealt with later. By the end of September Bomber Command as a whole had been trimmed to 33 front-line squadrons, or 480 aircraft, the rest, apart from two squadrons, being 'non-mobilisable' or in other words reserved to cover initial war wastage or the needs of operational training. The 23 squadrons which remained in Britain were organised as follows: six in 2 Group, based in East Anglia with Blenheim IVs; six in 3 Group, also in East Anglia with Wellington Is and IAs; five in 4 Group in Yorkshire with Whitley IIIs or IVs; and finally, six in 5 Group in Lincolnshire, with Hampdens. Thus at the outset only 17, ie the Wellingtons, Whitleys and Hampdens, were available for strategic bombing, the Blenheim's shorter range making it only suitable for tactical bombing.

Most of the existing war directives envisaged precision bombing, and due to grave doubts about the accuracy of night attack the bulk of Bomber Command was intended mainly as a day force from the very outset of the war. The sole exception, in fact, was 4 Group whose Whitleys, despite their superior range, were considerably slower than the other types and clearly sitting ducks in daylight.

The air warfare in Western Europe began on a cautious note, and this was to prevail throughout the period of the so-called 'phoney' war. Anxious to avoid using the RAF in any way that would provoke German retaliation on this country, the Government restricted air operations mostly to defensive patrolling, the only bombing which was permitted being the bombing of enemy warships at sea. As things stood, Bomber Command was in no shape to have conducted a successful strategic bombing offensive even if it had been allowed to do so, and the 'Phoney War' thus provided an opportunity for it to conserve its strength for the real 'shooting war' which was to come. Equally important, it enabled several long-held theories about war operations to be put to the test and, in particular, led to the decision to make Bomber Command primarily a night force.

Before describing Bomber Command's early operations it is of interest to note that had Germany suddenly begun unrestricted air action against Britain or France, the Command's directive demanded an immediate full-scale daylight assault on the Ruhr, which was believed to contain about sixty per cent of all Germany's vital industry and a population 'which might be expected to crack under intensive air attack'. Also necessary at this juncture, perhaps, is a word or two about the bombs which were available to Bomber Command in 1939. These were – like those of the enemy – basically very little different from their World War I counterparts, the only real difference perhaps being that they were of more streamlined form. The

RAF's standard 250lb and 500lb GP bombs were not only unsuited to the tasks for which they were used because of their general characteristics, which consisted of an unhappy compromise between strength of casing and weight of explosive, but they were relatively inefficient and all too frequently defective weapons. Their charge-weight ratio was only about 27 per cent as compared with the 50 per cent ratio of the German bombs, their explosive fillings were less efficient and many of the bombs failed to detonate. However, no serious attempt to remedy the situation was begun until the end of 1940 (by which time the 1,900lb GP bomb was also in use) and, as events proved, the development of bigger and better high explosive bombs – notably of the two new main types known as medium capacity (MC) and high-capacity (HC) – was slow.

Bomber Command launched its first offensive action on the afternoon of the second day of the war, when 15 Blenheim IVs from 107, 110 and 139 Squadrons and 14 Wellington Is from 9 and 149 Squadrons were detailed to attack German warships spotted by a Blenheim on reconnaissance that previous morning in Brunsbuttel, Wilhelmshaven and the Schillig Roads. Bad weather, fighter opposition and fierce anti-aircraft fire shielded the targets and altogether five Blenheims and two Wellingtons were lost. 139 Squadron's formation of five Blenheims failed to locate the enemy and returned to base. It was later learned that several of the Blenheim's 500lb General Purpose bombs hit the *Admiral von Scheer*, in the Schillig Roads, but failed to explode; being

A Vic formation of 149 Squadron's Wellington IAs on December 21, 1940, three days after the unit had been among those involved in the extremely costly attempt to bomb German warships in the Schillig Roads and Wilhelmshaven.

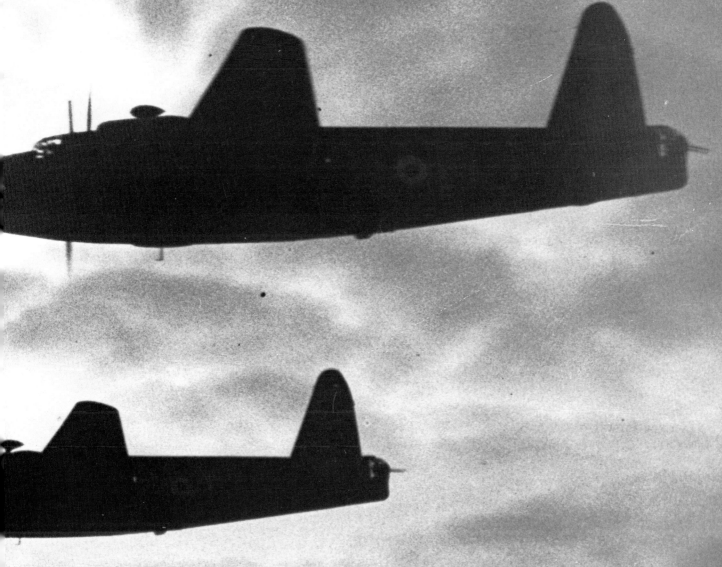

fused for 11 seconds delay they probably bounced overboard from the pocket battleship's armoured decks.

By the latter part of September 1939 it was deemed necessary to fly armed reconnaissance sweeps into the Heligoland Bight because experience since September 4 had shown that even if a single reconnaissance plane reported having sighted enemy warships at sea our bombers could not reach the spot in less than four hours, by which time the ships would have safely regained port. On September 29, during an armed sweep from Hemswell, 11 Hampdens of 144 Squadron found two destroyers near Heligoland, but lost five of their number to fighters from the North Frisian Isles. Of the section of six Hampdens that returned, only three reported having delivered attacks but results were not observed.

The next major operations came in December when, in an attempt to strike a major blow at the German fleet, 3 Group was ordered to take the first opportunity of making a high-altitude attack with at least 24 Wellington IAs (which had replaced the poorly-armed Mk Is), using 500lb Semi-Armour Piercing bombs, on an important enemy warship in the waters near Wilhelmshaven or Heligoland. Good weather was essential, to avoid any possibility of stray bombs falling on civilians, and the bombers were to operate in tight formations and rely for their protection upon collective fire-power.

The first two attacks, on the 3rd and 14th, were inconclusive, for although running fights with enemy fighters developed on both occasions the loss of six bombers on December 14 appeared to have been caused by flak. However, on December 18 when 24 Wellingtons from 9, 37 and 149 Squadrons attempted the third strike they came under heavy attack from 60 Messerschmitt Bf109s and 110s, and ship and shore anti-aircraft guns. The flak opened out some of the Wellington formations, and when the bombers had left Wilhelmshaven, after aiming some of their bombs at German warships, they were involved in a fierce running fight with the fighters until they were 70 or 80 miles out to sea on the homeward journey. The pilots of the German planes, which latter had been alerted by an experimental *Freya* early-warning radar station at Wangerooge, had already experienced the formidable rearward defences of the Wellington IA, and on this occasion they had been told to attack on the beam from above. In the event some did make beam attacks, whilst others came in from astern as before or else attacked simultaneously from the two rear quarters. The alarming result was that only 10 of the 22 Wellingtons returned. Most of the victims fell to beam attacks from above and were last seen in flames or with petrol pouring from their punctured fuel tanks. Two German fighters were shot down – both while making stern attacks.

The scale of this disaster, following as it did hard on that of December 14, was taken as a powerful warning of the superiority of the day fighter over the day bomber and the series of formation attacks was promptly abandoned. Immediate confidence in the theory of the self-defending formation, at least with the existing types of bomber, had been seriously shaken, though neither the idea nor the practice of daylight bombing was entirely shelved, and, indeed, were often to be revived in the future.

Following the debacle of December 18, the task of fitting the bombers with armoured and self-sealing fuel tanks proceeded apace, the Wellingtons also being provided with beam machine tuns.

Although Germany's air defences by day had proved themselves far more formidable than expected, at night it seemed that they had no counterpart. From the very outset of the war 4 Group's ponderous Whitleys were engaged almost continuously on nocturnal propaganda leaflet-dropping and reconnaissance missions over the Nazi homeland, yet enemy reaction was minimal; fighter opposition was totally absent and the few flak guns and searchlights that were encountered proved comparatively ineffective. The leaflets – which were carried in bundles held together by elastic bands and released either from the Whitley's 'dustbin' turret or the flare chute, whereupon they broke loose on hitting the slipstream – were code named *Nickels* and the operations thus became *Nickelling*. The disgusted Whitley crews, deprived as they were of dropping bombs owing to government policy, preferred to call their missions 'bumph raids', clearly confirming their personal opinion of the real purpose they served!

After the war Bomber Command's famous wartime AOC-in-C Sir Arthur Harris (he was AOC 5 Group during the 'phoney' war) acidly commented that the only practical result of dropping leaflets was 'to supply the Continent's requirements of toilet paper', although he, like many others, admitted that the operations gave useful training to the crews. The long flights, which began on the first night of the war when Whitleys of 51 and 58 Squadrons visited Hamburg, Bremen and the Ruhr, were certainly of considerable importance in giving the first experience of long-range night flying at high altitudes over a blacked-out hostile territory. The crews' worst enemy during that first wartime winter was the appalling weather. Very often the bombers' wings and fuselages became so heavily coated with ice that it became difficult to maintain height. Heating systems – then rather primitive and inadequate at the best of times – would often fail and crews would suffer acute pain, and very often frostbite, from the severe cold at high altitudes. Sometimes thick ice formed inside the cockpit and the instruments froze. Oxygen bottles were known to freeze to crew members' fingers and, on occasion, the oxygen systems failed too. A strange phenomenon seen on many flights was the eerie light of St Elmo's fire playing about the wing tips, propellers and guns; sometimes the entire aircraft would be outlined in violet light, sparks would fly from

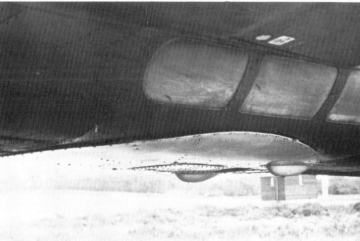

Top: Whitley IIIs of the type which made Bomber Command's first wartime penetrations into Germany pictured shortly before the war. On the machine in the background the lowered 'dustbin' turret can be seen.

Left/Above: The two-gun 'dustbin' ventral turret common to the Whitley III, IV and IVA shown extended and retracted. This particular installation was photographed on Whitley III K7183 at the A&AEE Martlesham Heath in May 1938./*via Raymond Williams*

one point to another, and every movement of the crew crackled in the electric air.

Typical of the experience of the Whitley crews is the following account of a flight on October 27, 1939 by the crew of 51 Squadron Whitley III K8989 detailed to drop leaflets on Munich; the aircraft was operating from an advanced base at Villeneuve in France, was captained by Flg Off H. Budden, and had the squadron's CO, Wg Cdr J. Silvester, aboard as second pilot. Crystalline icing was encountered above 20,000ft in cloud. The temperature was –22C. The front gun was frozen and the centre trimming tabs jammed. The mid guns jammed shortly afterwards. Oxygen was necessary, but only one bottle was charged, the others being empty. The temperature dropped to –30C. At 14,900ft the ice accretion had dropped but temperature had fallen to the temperature gauge limit. At 2015hr the oxygen supply ran out, but course was set direct to the point 42 miles NE of Munich. The leaflets were dropped at 18,800ft by hand down the flare chute. Such was the condition of the navigator and wireless operator at this stage that every few minutes they were compelled to lie down and rest on the floor of the fuselage. The cockpit heating system was useless. Everyone was frozen, and had no means of alleviating their distress. The front gunner lay in a heap on the floor, utterly exhausted. The navigator and the commanding officer were butting their heads on the floor and navigation table in an endeavour to experience some form of pain as a relief from frostbite and lack of oxygen. This crew had had no food since midday and

were not supplied with any before take-off about 1800hr.

On October 1/2 4 Group's Whitleys dropped leaflets on Berlin for the first time, and early in 1940 they ranged as far afield as Prague and Vienna. 5 Group's Hampdens were by now taking a share of the *Nickel* raids, and in March came the first damaging encounter with a German night fighter. The same month also saw leaflets dropped on Poland, by Whitleys, and it was during the second trip to that country, on the night of 15/16th, that the crew of 77 Squadron Whitley V N1387 'L-Love', captained by Flt Lt Tomlin, performed a feat which probably equalled, if not surpassed, the best 'line-shoot' made by a RAF crew during the entire war. They had been flying for eleven hours by dead-reckoning when, after battling with a headwind on the return journey from Warsaw to Villeneuve, they had to land. Unfortunately, by error, they landed in Germany and although their story – like the many other classics concerning the 'bumphleteering' Whitleys – has been oft told before, the following contemporary account, by BBC war correspondent Charles Gardner, is not well known and surely merits an airing:

'This is the full story of the amazing adventure of the two young British pilots who landed in Germany to ask

A bundle of leaflets goes down the flare chute of a Whitley V of 102 Squadron./*IWM*

the way – and who then stayed on German territory for
quarter of an hour, before taking-off again and getting
safely back to France.

'The pilots – one a flight lieutenant and the other a
flying officer – were in a British bomber which had
been night flying. On the way back they ran into a
strong headwind and had to climb to 18,000ft over a
layer of cloud; the climbing and the headwind took up
a lot of petrol, with the result that they began to run
short. It was still dark, but they decided that they were
certain to be over French territory, so they came down
through the clouds – which incidentally were on to the
hill tops – and circled round at 500ft. They could see
one or two villages and a town with factory chimneys, a
place they estimated of about 25,000 inhabitants.

'Then, as our plane was looking for a field, an anti-
aircraft gun fired a warning shot, so the flight lieutenant
put on his navigation lights, gave a recognition signal,
and put down his wheels – and there was no more
firing. Still thinking he was over France, the pilot chose
his field and landed in it, unloaded the plane's guns,
stopped the engines and, with the flying officer, got out
of the machine. At the other end of the field they could
see a group of peasants running towards them and they
went out to meet them, which they did about 200
yards from the plane. The flying officer spoke to the
leader of the peasant group and said chattily, "C'est
France, n'est pas?" The peasant just looked at him,
and shook his head. The flying officer tried again and
said encouragingly, "Luxembourg alors?". Another
head-shake, but this time the peasant pointed to one of

The 77 Squadron Whitley which, as described in the text, landed
in Germany in error and got away in the nick of time pictured
afterwards with its crew./*IWM*

his friends and said "Hans Franzosich", meaning
that Hans spoke French. So Hans was asked, "C'est
France, n'est pas?" To which he replied in a strong
German accent, but very politely, "Non, Monsieur,
c'est l'Allemagne, la frontiere est a vingt kilometres,"
and obligingly he pointed out the direction in which
France lay.

'I think the next few seconds are best described by the
flight lieutenant – when he said, "Like one man we
turned and bolted for the machine". Remember it was
200 yards away and the engines were stopped, but they
made it, I should guess in about even time, just as a
group of other figures started running up from the far
end of the field. It says something for British engines
that those of our bomber didn't let them down, they
started straight away, and our plane just roared out of
that field without, as one of the crew said, "stopping
even to say thank you to the peasants." The rear
gunner in the bomber reported that the newcomers
opened fire as the plane was taking off, but they didn't
hit. Also someone fired off what looked to be like red
Verey lights, but they didn't do any damage either.

'Luckily there was still enough petrol in the tanks to
get the plane over that 25 kilometres to the frontier, but
this time the pilots didn't try to land until they were
dead sure it was a bit of France underneath. They got

their check from seeing in the growing light a hoarding advertising a popular French drink and put down again. Even so, when they did land, four of the crew stayed in the plane with their engines running and the guns loaded while the flying officer went off to make sure.'

In November 1939 German U-boats and aircraft began laying magnetic mines close inshore to Britain to harry our shipping. The aircraft responsible for this new menace were mostly Heinkel He 115 seaplanes based on Borkum, Sylt and Nordeney, and as a counter-measure Bomber Command instituted armed 'Security Patrols' over the bases to discourage the Heinkels from taking off. These patrols began on December 12/13, and were flown nightly at low level by single aircraft operating in relays. Crews were forbidden to attack land objectives although sometimes the waterborne flarepath and seaplanes alighting or taking-off were bombed and machine-gunned.

Initially the patrols, which proved quite effective, were flown by 4 Group's Whitleys but from late February 1940 until early May 1940, when they ended, they were flown by 5 Group's Hampdens.

On March 19/20, 1940 the seaplane base at Hornum on the island of Sylt was the target for the first British air attack of the war on a land target. The raid was mounted as a reprisal for an attack by 15 German bombers on the fleet anchorage at Scapa Flow three nights previously, when we suffered our first civilian air raid casualties. Thirty Whitleys of 4 Group and 20 Hampdens of 5 Group were despatched – all with experienced crews who had knowledge of the target area – and the attack was delivered by moonlight over a period of six hours, the first four hours being alloted to the Whitleys and the remaining two to the Hampdens. 500lb and 250lb GP bombs were carried and certain specially selected aircraft also carried incendiaries in the hope that fires would be started which would help to mark the target; some aircraft also carried flares. Twenty-six Whitleys and 15 Hampdens claimed to have attacked the target, the attacks being delivered singly at short intervals from heights varying from 10,000 to 1,000ft. All the bomb-aimers reported that the target was easily recognisable and many direct hits on the seaplane base were claimed. As each bomber approached Sylt a semi-circle of searchlight beams sprang into the sky, and a heavy barrage of flak was put up. One pilot said: 'We were closely followed by a trail of pom-pom shells. At one stage they were too close for comfort. Our first bomb hit the ground near a slipway, and three others, according to a pilot of a machine which was close behind, registered hits on a hangar.' Another pilot, whose Whitley approached Sylt at about 1,500 feet, reported: 'We flew round and identified the targets and then dived to one thousand feet over them. My second pilot, who acted as bomb-aimer, directed me on the target, and we had just flown over

Above: A drawback of the Hampden's narrow fuselage was that if the pilot was killed or wounded it was impossible for another crew member to remove him from his seat and take over the controls.

Right: Crew of a 5 Group Hampden are greeted by the ground staff on return to their base in Lincolnshire after the bombing raid on Hornum on the night of March 19/20, 1940.

it when suddenly I heard a shout from behind, "We have hit them."'

Only one aircraft – a Whitley – failed to return from this operation, which was the first attack aimed by Bomber Command against a land target. It was the portent of a mighty offensive. But what at first seemed, from the crew reports, to have been an encouraging start was quickly disproved by a photographic reconnaissance of Sylt, which showed that all the buildings at Hornum remained 'outwardly intact'. Night bombing was obviously going to be more difficult than expected, but Bomber Command knew, from 3 Group's experiences in December 1939, that a return to heavy day bombing was right out of the question until more advanced aircraft entered service.

During the month of the Hornum raid Bomber Command Headquarters, which had moved from its original home at Uxbridge to Ritchings Park, near Langley, Bucks in August 1939, was relocated at Naphill just outside High Wycombe, where it was to remain for the rest of its existence. 1940 also saw two changes of C-in-Cs. In April Air Marshal C. F. A. Portal assumed command from Sir Edgar Ludlow Hewitt (who had succeeded the original C-in-C, Sir John Steel in September 1937), and in October 1940, he in turn was succeeded by Sir Richard Peirse.

Operations: Meeting the German Attack

The 'Phoney War' suddenly ended on April 8/9 with the German invasion of Denmark and Norway, and although Bomber Command entered the campaign it could give the hard-pressed ground forces no more than limited help as it was still earmarked to oppose any sudden enemy move against France. Such raids as were made were directed chiefly against enemy-held airfields in southern Norway and were made by forces of up to twelve aircraft; they were thus merely pin-pricks and had no appreciable effect on the military situation whatever.

Even so, these missions, which were flown both by night and day – and in generally foul weather – were not without cost to Bomber Command, the heaviest losses in any single operation being suffered on April 12 when twelve Hampdens of 44 and 50 Squadrons tried to attack a warship in Kristiansand. Caught by German fighters, and having no defence against a beam attack, they were 'hacked down from the wing man inwards' until half their number had perished.

Harris, in command of 5 Group, was fully aware that the Hampden was cold meat for any determined enemy fighter in daylight for, to use his own words:* '[it] was then a most feebly armed aircraft with a single gun on top and a single one underneath, manned by a gunner in a hopelessly cramped position, together with a gun firing forward which, as it was fixed, was of no value at all. The mounts of the two moveable guns were rickety and had a limited traverse with many blind spots'. Anxious to get something done to improve matters with the least possible delay, Harris 'collected a technically minded Station commander' in his Group, E. A. B. Rice, and visited Messrs Alfred Rose and Sons, 'a typically English "family" firm' at Gainsborough. Within a fortnight this manufacturing firm produced designs for gun mountings which eliminated the disabilities of the original type, doubled the Hampden's effective fire power and greatly reduced the blind spots.

Bomber Offensive (Collins) 1947

A few weeks later the gun mountings were in full production and going into action, yet if they had been
ordered through the normal channels they would very
probably never have materialised. When Harris was
asked why he had ordered two thousand of these
mountings without authority to do so he replied 'If I
had ordered twenty or two hundred I should have had
to pay for them myself, and that anyhow they were
necessary – as indeed they were.'

During this period, on the night of April 13/14 to be
precise, sea-mining – which was to grow into one of

Before the storm : A Blenheim IV of 139 Squadron in France
during the winter of 1939-40./*IWM*

Bomber Command's regular duties – began when twelve Hampdens of 5 Group laid mines off the Danish coast. Mining, or *Gardening* as it was code-named, was held to be the duty of Coastal Command, but due to early problems with Beaufort aircraft, it could not fulfil the task. The mines employed at this time were converted naval types weighing 15,000lb and dropped by parachute. It was very difficult to fit them into aircraft and the Hampden alone of the existing 'heavies' had suitable stowage.

Denmark was quickly occupied by the Germans almost without effort, and by early May the Allies were compelled by events in France to leave Norway to its fate – a fate greatly facilitated all along by the action of the *Luftwaffe*. An element of Bomber Command – 1 Group – had, it will be recalled, been despatched to France on the day before the outbreak of war, and become known as the initial element of the Advanced Air Striking Force. Ten squadrons strong, it was deployed on airfields and landing grounds in the Rheims area – heart of the champagne country – and was originally intended as the forward-based element of the RAF's strategic attack force, based so close to Germany that even its short-range Battle day bombers would be able to deal heavy blows against enemy airfields and industry. To this end, on their arrival in France, on the eve of the war, the Battles were immediately refuelled and loaded with bombs stockpiled some time earlier under the guise of a sale to the French Air Force. In the event it never did any strategic bombing, and its initial task was photographic reconnaissance to a depth of some 10 or 20 miles over the Franco-German frontier. The 241mph Battle aircraft, fast as it may have seemed when it first flew in 1936, was now, however, hopelessly outpaced by the 354mph Bf109E and, equally, its armament of one fixed and one movable machine gun was no match for the Messerschmitt's twin 20mm cannon and machine-guns. Proof of its shortcomings came on September 29 when five aircraft of 150 Squadron – an entire formation – was shot down by Bf109s. Following this incident the reconnaissance missions were temporarily halted and, in a desperate attempt to beef-up the Battles' defensive armament, rear guns which fired back and downwards were hurriedly installed. 12 Squadron's diarist recorded that his squadron's 'lash-up' of this kind was not very successful as the observer

Below: A Battle of 142 Squadron in France during the 'Phoney War' When the German breakthrough came Battle losses soon began to mount alarmingly; on May 11, for example, when eight Battles from 88 and 218 Squadrons were sent to attack a troop column in Germany, only one returned./*IWM*

Right: To help defend the Blenheim IV from fighter attack from below, a single hand-operated rearward-firing gun was fitted beneath the nose, and as this July 1940 line up of machines from 110 (VE) 15 (LS) and UX (82) Squadrons shows there were several distinct types of installations; the standard installation featured a transparent Perspex housing as seen on the third Blenheim from the camera. VE-A (R3741), nearest camera, also features a fixed, remotely-controlled rearward-firing .303in gun in the topside of the port nacelle, this being a squadron 'lash-up'. /*IWM*

Below right: Armourers at Linton-on-Ouse, Yorks, prepare to load 500lb and 250lb general-purpose bombs into a Whitley V of 58 Squadron in mid 1940. Towing the bomb trolleys is a Fordson tractor, while in the background can be seen a Crossley IGL 3-ton lorry and a Humber utility./*IWM*

had to stand with his back to the gun, and fire it by bending down and aiming it between his legs!

The winter of 1939/40 in Europe was the coldest for half a century – at Boulogne the Channel froze – and by December conditions at the AASF airfields in France, which were often no more than large meadows, were so bad that flying was impossible. Two of the Battle squadrons (15 and 40) were withdrawn to England during the month to rearm with Blenheims and to take their place came 114 and 139 Blenheim Squadrons, from 2 Group, It was so cold that even tins of anti-freezing mixture were frozen solid and although little tents were rigged up round the Battles' and Blenheims' engines and stores put in the tents, this often was to no avail. Nevertheless, engines *were* somehow coaxed into life and practice flying continued with the temperature at 40 degrees below zero. Some night flying was done at this time and various dive-bombing and fighter-evasion tactics were tried.

March brought the thaw – and the mud. And it also saw the bombers detached for short-range reconnaissance-cum-leaflet raids to ease the strain on the heavies of Bomber Command at home.

At dawn on May 8 the German onslaught on the Low Countries and France began, and after a seemingly interminable delay caused by the obstinacy of the French Generalissimo, the Battles and Blenheims were sent into action against advancing columns of enemy troops. As no fighter escort was available the Battles were told to approach their targets at 250 feet using bombs fused for 11 seconds' delay. They encountered a storm of ground fire and by nightfall on that first day 13 of the 32 Battles sent into action had been lost. Three days later, when eight Battles of 88 and 218 Squadrons were sent to bomb a troop column in Germany, only one pilot returned – and he doubted whether any crew had reached their target, having

seen three of his companions succumb to ground fire in the Ardennes. On the same day 114 (Blenheim) Squadron was almost completely wiped out when its airfield was attacked by the *Luftwaffe*, and on the 12th 139 Squadron lost seven of its nine Blenheims when they ran into a swarm of enemy fighters.

In one of the most heroic actions of the entire campaign, five Battle crews of 12 Squadron flew to virtually certain death on May 10, in an attempt to destroy two German-held road bridges over the Albert Canal near Maastricht in Belgium. None returned, but one bridge was put out of action and the leader of the raid, Flg Off D. E. Garland and his observer, Sgt T. Gray, received posthumously the first Victoria Crosses awarded to the RAF in World War II.

Between May 10 and mid-day on May 14, the serviceable strength of the AASF bomber squadrons dwindled from 135 to 71. In the afternoon of May 14 all 71 survivors were called upon for a final last-ditch effort to try to halt the German troops massed for the break-through at Sedan. Strong forces of Bf109s were encountered and 40 bombers did not return – the highest rate of loss ever experienced by the RAF in an operation on such a scale. In the evening when 28

Below: The W/T operator in a Wellington I of 215 Squadron hands a message to the second pilot in April 1940, when the aircraft was on temporary loan to 75 (New Zealand) Squadron for a special long-range reconnaissance sortie to Narvik in Norway. In the left foreground the navigator's table may be seen./*IWM*

Right: To the back of beyond. Taken at a gunnery school 'somewhere in England' in the summer of 1940, this picture shows a rear gunner sliding over the top of the retracted Frazer-Nash ventral 'dustbin' turret in a Wellington to take up his position in the rear turret. The twin-gun ventral turret was fitted to the Mk IA and early Mk IC Wellingtons but was not installed on subsequent aircraft because it caused c.g. problems.

Blenheims of Bomber Command continued the attack they lost seven of their number.

The AASF now gradually withdrew, continuing its grim struggle as it did so until France's inevitable collapse. During this final phase the Battles operated mainly by night and suffered few losses, while the Blenheims joined the reconnaissance Blenheims of the Air Component of the British Expeditionary Force. 'Flying and landing a Battle at night', comments the *RAF Short Official History* 'was no easy task – there was a brilliant glare from the exhaust which dazzled the pilot, and the view from the observer's seat was poor – but those difficulties which were not overcome were ignored, and there was an immediate and dramatic decline in the casualty rate. During the intense daylight operations of May 10-14, one aircraft had been lost in every two sorties; during the night operations of May 20-June 4 the loss was just over one in every two hundred.' Night bombing, however, was by no means all gain, for safety could only be achieved at the expense of accuracy. In fact, so many Battle crews now dropped their bombs with no more precise identifications of their targets than that provided by watches, that Air Marshal A. S. Barratt, the AOC-in-C British Air Forces in France, was compelled to forbid bombing on 'estimated time of arrival'. Thereafter, the phrase ceased to appear in the pilots' reports, but even so the practice continued.

Left: A Blenheim IV of 107 Squadron (not 101 as previously reported), with serial number and codes 'OM' removed by the censor, pictured over a burning British or French ship which was destroyed by German attacks off Bordeaux in May 1940. (Contemporary captions claimed that the ship was the Blenheim's victim, but although this was untrue it still made a good wartime propaganda picture). Of special interest is the Vickers K-type gas-operated gun seen protruding from the tail, just aft of the tailwheel – a 'lash-up' exclusive to 107 Squadron aircraft./IWM

Below: German troops run for cover as a Fairey Battle strafes their column of horse-drawn vehicles in May 1940 during the invasion of France./IWM

Bomber Command aircraft based in Britain also operated over the battle area from the start of the campaign, the first attacks being launched on May 10 by Blenheims, and during the night Wellingtons. Attacks which would have caused the death of German civilians were still forbidden by the War Cabinet but as a matter of military necessity action by some Whitleys at the AASF's request against communications in Germany east of the Rhine was not ruled out. Thus it was that on the night of May 10/11 eight Whitleys of 77 and 102 Squadrons made Bomber Command's first bombing raid against the German mainland, when they attacked roads, railways and bridges in and near Geldern, Goch, Cleve and Wesel on the enemy's route to southern Holland. On the following night, again at the request of the AASF, the first *large* attack on the German mainland was made. The target was the communications radiating from the important railway junction of Munchen-Gladbach, and the attackers Whitleys of 51, 58, 77 and 102 Squadrons and Hampdens of 44, 49, 50, 61 and 144 Squadrons. Thirty-six aircraft were despatched, five Hampdens returned early and about half the remaining aircraft bombed the target. One Whitley and two Hampdens failed to return but both Hampden crews, less one pilot, made their way to the Allied lines.

At last, on May 15, the War Cabinet authorised Bomber Command to extend its operations from the battle zones and their immediate lines of communication, to targets in Germany east of the Rhine and strategic bombing finally began. That night 93 aircraft of Bomber Command took off to bomb oil targets and railway centres in the Ruhr and a similar operation was mounted the following night.

The immediate aim of this sudden change of policy was to sting the enemy into diverting his air strength against England rather than France. By this time, however, the pressing needs of the land battle resulted in some of the heavies' effort being switched back to a tactical role and they remained divided between strategic and close-support operations until the fall of France.

The Blenheims of 2 Group, in common with the AASF's Battles, were fully engaged in impeding the German advance throughout the campaign. Like the Battles, they had long been obsolete, and although most pilots considered them pleasant to fly – buoyant, aerobatic, and light on the controls – they now possessed neither the armament necessary to a slow bomber nor the speed necessary to an unarmed bomber. Consequently, in formation they proved highly vulnerable, as was demonstrated by a grim encounter on May 17 when 82 Squadron was ordered to attack German columns near Gembloux. The twelve Blenheims were approaching the target at 8,000ft when a burst of flak promptly claimed one victim and the formation began to open out. Fifteen Bf109s then closed in and only one of the original twelve Blenheims survived the combat, and even that one was heavily damaged. The immediate reaction to this disaster was that the Blenheims were confined to night operations, but shortly afterwards when the full extent of the threat to the British Expeditionary Force became clear the decision was reversed – albeit with the proviso that unless good cloud cover could be relied upon, the bombers were to have fighter escort.

During the evacuation from Dunkirk Bomber Command gave valuable assistance to the ground forces striving to prevent the enemy from reaching the beaches, but thereafter the small force available and the inexperience of many of its crews prevented it from intervening with any decisive effect in the swift course of events in France. Italy entered the war at this stage, and on the night of June 11/12, less than 24 hours after she had done so, 36 Whitleys of 10, 51, 58, 77 and 102 Squadrons, which had refuelled in the Channel Islands, set out to attack industrial objectives in Turin and Genoa. The raid proved largely abortive; only ten claimed to have bombed Turin and two more the alternative, Genoa. One Whitley failed to return. The other twenty-three found the heavy storms, low cloud and severe icing conditions over the Alps, too much for them and returned early. In the case of Whitley V P4957 of 10 Squadron, captained by Sqn Ldr Hanafin, the aircraft was struck by lightning and had to abandon the mission as a result of shock to the rear gunner who had been leaning on his guns, and burns to the wireless operator. Twelve Wellingtons which had also been detailed to bomb Italy did not take-off at all. They had flown from England to an advanced base at Salon in the south of France early in the day, but the French, fearful of provoking the Italians to retaliation, prevented the bombers from taking off. Several days later the French relented and allowed Salon airfield to be used, but the capitulation of France prevented the development of heavy raids on Italy for a long time.

The six weeks of the Battle of France cost Bomber Command 340 aircraft, although only 69 of these were heavies. 1 Group – the AASF – was almost completely wiped out and although, on July 1, 1940, the remnants of the squadrons that had been withdrawn from France on June 15 could still officially muster some 70 Battles, these machines were replaced as soon as possible by Wellingtons, the best of the heavies, the production of which was accelerated. At this date the Command's effective strength lay in approximately 200 Blenheims, 110 Hampdens, 100 Whitleys and 150 Wellingtons, not all of which were, however, available on a day-to-day basis.

Above right: Ground crew examine a battle-damaged Blenheim IV of 110 Squadron in 1940./*IWM*

Right: Twin Vickers K gun installations in the upper and lower rear positions of a Hampden of 83 Squadron, Scampton, Lincs, in 1940. Note the open side entrance to the lower gun position.

Bomber Command Order of Battle – April 11, 1940

Unit	Parent Station	Establishment	Aircraft	Remarks
2 Group	WYTON			
107 Sqn	Wattisham	16* + 5†	Blenheim IV	Operational
110 Sqn	Wattisham	16* + 5†	Blenheim IV	Operational
21 Sqn	Watton	16* + 5†	Blenheim IV	Operational
82 Sqn	Wattisham	16* + 5†	Blenheim IV	Operational
40 Sqn	Wyton	16* + 5†	Blenheim IV	Operational
15 Sqn	Wattisham	16* + 5†	Blenheim IV	Operational
101 Sqn	W. Raynham	27*	Blenheim IV	Reserve Sqn
3 Group	EXNING			
99 Sqn	Newmarket	16*	Wellington 1A & 1C	Operational
149 Sqn	Mildenhall	16*	Wellington 1A & 1C	Operational
38 Sqn	Marham	16*	Wellington 1A & 1C	Operational
115 Sqn	Marham	16*	Wellington 1A & 1C	Operational
9 Sqn	Honington	16*	Wellington 1A & 1C	Operational
215 Sqn	Honington	?	Wellington 1A & 1C	Re-forming
37 Sqn	Feltwell	16*	Wellington 1A & 1C	Operational
75 (NZ)	Feltwell	16*	Wellington 1A & 1C	Operational
214 Sqn	Stradishall	24*	Wellington 1 & 1A	Reserve Sqn
4 Group	YORK			
51 Sqn	Dishforth	16*	Whitley IV & V	Operational
58 Sqn	Linton	16*	Whitley III & V	Operational
10 Sqn	Dishforth	16*	Whitley IV & V	Operational
77 Sqn	Driffield	16*	Whitley V	Operational
102 Sqn	Driffield	16*	Whitley V	Operational
78 Sqn	Linton-on-Ouse	24*	Whitley IVA & V	Reserve Sqn
5 Group	GRANTHAM			
61 Sqn	Hemswell	16*	Hampden	Operational
144 Sqn	Hemswell	16*	Hampden	Operational
49 Sqn	Scampton	16*	Hampden	Operational
83 Sqn	Scampton	16*	Hampden	Operational
44 Sqn	Waddington	16*	Hampden	Operational
50 Sqn	Waddington	16*	Hampden	Operational
106 Sqn	Finningley	24*	Hampden	Reserve Sqn
185 Sqn	Cottesmore	?	Hampden	Re-forming
6 (Training) Group	ABINGDON			
207 Sqn	Cranfield	24* + 8†	Battle , Anson	Group pool for BAFF.
98 Sqn	Finningley	21*	Battle	Reserve Sqn for BAFF
10 OTU	Abingdon	Absorbs 97 & 166 Sqns	Whitley II & III & Anson	
11 OTU	Bassingbourn	Absorbs 215 Sqn	Wellington	
12 OTU	Benson	Absorbs 52 & 63 Sqns	Battle	
13 OTU	Bicester	Absorbs 104 & 108 Sqns	Blenheim I & IV , & Anson	
14 OTU	Cottesmore	Absorbs 185 Sqn	Hampden & Hereford	
15 OTU	Harwell	Absorbs 75 & 148 Sqns	Wellington I & Anson	
16 OTU	Upper Heyford	Absorbs 7 & 76 Sqns	Hampden & Anson	
17 OTU	Upwood	Absorbs 90 & 35 Sqns	Blenheim I & IV , & Anson	
18 OTU	Hucknall	Polish	12 Battles	
19 OTU	Hawarden			
20 OTU	Lichfield			
21 OTU	Cranfield	Soon to absorb 207 Sqn now at Cottesmore	Battle & Anson	

*Initial Establishment   †Initial Reserve

Operations: The Battle of Britain and the Early Strategic Offensive

Britain now had to fight on alone and the C-in-C Bomber Command, Air Marshal Portal, was anxious to begin in earnest the task of striking strategic blows against Germany's vitals, with the ulterior aim of gradually undermining her from within. 'In Bomber Command', he declared in July 1940, 'we have the one directly offensive weapon in the whole of our armoury, the one means by which we can undermine the morale of a large part of the enemy people, shake their faith in the Nazi regime and at the same time dislocate the major part of their heavy industry, much of their chemical industry and a good part of their oil production.'

It had already been decided that the main effort should be against the German aircraft industry, the oil industry and communications, but in fact this was once again frequently diverted to meet a more pressing need – this time the need to reduce the threat of invasion of Britain by striking against the invasion ports and shipping. At first the Blenheims of 2 Group were sent to attack airfields and ports in the Low Countries, targets which were also given to the Hampdens, Wellingtons and Whitleys as secondary objectives to those in Germany, but by mid-September the entire bomber force (including the remaining Battles) was attacking invasion targets – the ships in harbour, the communications behind the ports, the gun emplacements on the coast. The bombers went forth to the Channel ports night after night, and as there was no difficulty in finding the targets, and because the short distance enabled maximum bomb loads to be carried, good results were obtained.

A vivid impression of a successful attack at this time was written soon afterwards by Flg Off R. S. Gilmour, the pilot of a Blenheim. His target was Ostend and as he approached it the whole of 'Blackpool Front', as the

Crew of a Blenheim IV of 40 Squadron await the take-off signal at RAF Wyton, Hunts, on July 25, 1940. The Blenheim possessed neither the armament necessary to a slow bomber, nor the speed necessary to an unarmed bomber and, consequently, the squadrons suffered heavy losses during their daylight operations in 1940. Between May 9 and June 4 the Blenheims of 2 Group completed 856 daylight sorties and lost 56 aircraft, in addition to a further 10 damaged beyond repair. At one period in those same two hectic months 40 Squadron lost two COs within eight days./*IWM*

crews dubbed the invasion coastline stretching west from Dunkirk, was in view. Calais docks and the Boulogne waterfront were on fire and glares extended for miles. 'The whole French coast seemed to be a barrier of flame broken only by intense white flashes of exploding bombs and vari-coloured incendiary tracers soaring and circling skywards.'

Gilmour dived towards his target and felt a surging kick on the control column as the bombs left the plane. 'A second later the bomb-aimer was through to me on the 'phones . . . "Bombs gone" '.

German records show that, of the vessels assembled for the invasion of Britain, 21 transports, 214 barges and five tugs had been sunk or damaged by September 21. These losses, in themselves, had no significant effect on the enemy's plans as is sometimes claimed. Nevertheless, Bomber Command did make a critical contribution to the outcome of the Battle of Britain – albeit unconsciously – by driving, in conjunction with the Royal Navy, the enemy to seek battle with RAF Fighter Command in order to try to gain air superiority over the Channel and southern England. Without achieving mastery of the air he knew only too well that both Bomber Command and our greatly superior naval forces would be able to offer very stiff opposition to the invading German armies. But if he gained the upper hand in the air he could put the bombers and warships to the sword.

It was during this critical period of 1940 that the German town of Hamm frequently figured in the news, for it had the largest railway marshalling yards in Germany. Standing at the north-east corner of the Ruhr it regulated, in conjunction with Osnabruck, Soest and Schwerke, nearly all the rail traffic between the Ruhr and Central and Eastern Germany. To the bomber crews it became known as the 'Ham and Egg' run, 'egg' being RAF slang for a bomb.

In theory, marshalling yards should have presented easy targets for bombers, due to the fact that much sorting of rolling stock was done at night and signal lights were essential. But although Hamm and many rail centres came in for attack, little appreciable effect on the running of the railways resulted, for the weight of the attacks was still too puny and, furthermore, the enemy's repair organisation was extremely efficient.

Enemy opposition was, on the whole, slight on these early raids. Heavy flak was seldom encountered and as yet few German night fighters sought to intercept the bombers. As a rule the worst hazards were still the elements – dense cloud, bitterly cold and constantly

changing winds at the higher altitudes, and often low cloud, fog or mist on the return trip across the North Sea after some eight or nine hours' flying. Many lives and aircraft were lost through crews losing their way and running short of fuel, or due to other difficulties.

An unusual operation performed by 5 Group at this time was an attack on August 12/13 against a much more satisfactory bottleneck than Hamm – the Dortmund-Ems canal, which formed one of the two main outlets to the sea for Ruhr coal, manufactured goods and invasion craft. It was vulnerable at the point where it is carried across the river Ems by two aqueducts, and ten Hampden crews of 49 and 83 Squadrons had made several dummy attacks in moonlight on canals in Lincolnshire in preparation for the dangerous mission. In the actual raid five Hampdens created a diversion by attacking adjacent lock gates and river craft, while the remaining five bombers attacked one of the two heavily-defended aqueducts. The aqueduct in question – it carried the older arm of the canal, the new branch having been considerably damaged in earlier raids – was heavily protected by flak guns cunningly dispersed so as to form a lane down which an attacking aircraft had to fly, if it was to reach the target.

All five Hampdens carried 1,000lb bombs, the first time that this weapon was used operationally by the RAF, and attacked singly at two-minute intervals from very low level. The first machine was hit and the wireless operator wounded; the second was hit and destroyed. The third was set on fire but the pilot managed to gain sufficient height for the crew to bale out before the bomber became uncontrollable; all were captured. The fourth Hampden was hit in three places but got back to base. The fifth one, captained by Flight

Lieutenant R. A. B. Learoyd of 49 Squadron, flew down the flak lane at 200ft. 'After a moment', said Learoyd, 'three big holes appeared in the starboard wing. They were firing at point-blank range. The navigator continued to direct me on to the target. I could not see it because I was blinded by the glare of the searchlights and had to keep my head above the cockpit top. At last I heard the navigator say "Bombs gone"; I immediately did a steep turn to the right and got away, being fired at heavily for five minutes. The carrier pigeon we carried laid an egg during the attack'. Learoyd then discovered that the hydraulic system had been severely damaged, so that the flaps and the undercarriage mechanism would not work. When he reached his base at Scampton, he circled the airfield until the approaching dawn enabled him to see the ground to make a belly landing. This he accomplished safely. When the target was photographed next day it was seen that a large part of the aqueduct had been blown away and the canal had been drained. Learoyd was awarded the Victoria Cross.

Another noteworthy operation in August 1940 was the first bombing raid on Berlin, on the 25/26th, in reply to the initial *Luftwaffe* raid on central London the night before. Eighty-one Wellingtons, Whitleys and Hampdens were despatched and they were detailed to attack various industrial objectives in the city. Twenty-nine crews claimed to have bombed the German capital, most of the others being unable to find their targets because of thick cloud. Five aircraft failed to return, three of them ditching in the sea and their crews being rescued.

In September the code word *Razzling* frequently appeared in the Operational Orders, this signifying fire-raising attacks with incendiary leaves (code-named *Razzle* or in a larger version *Decker*). Targets were the Black, the Thuringen and Grunewald forests and the wooded slopes of the Hartz mountains where military stores were thought to be concealed. 4 Group's Whitleys were among the bombers engaged in these missions, and the Operations Record Book (Form 540) of 10 Squadron, based at Leeming, Yorks, describes the incendiary device as a sheet of raw rubber between two sheets of celluloid, to which was affixed a sheet of phosphorous. The incendiary leaves were an American invention and were stored in cans of water to prevent them from igniting in the air and, when the target was reached, were poured down the flare chute, ordinary garden syringes being provided to squirt water down the flare chute to unstick any remaining ones.

Only limited success was achieved with these weapons. Some crews reported explosions in the target areas, apparently as a result of ammunition dumps being fired, while from abroad came amusing tales of German souvenir hunters putting the leaves in their trousers pockets where they burst into flame! On the debit side, three Whitley tailplanes were destroyed at Leeming alone, when incendiary leaves stuck to the aircraft in flight but did not ignite until the blast of the slipstream had died away; they burst into flames as the bombers taxied in.

By the end of October the Battle of Britain had been won and with the immediate threat of invasion lifted, Bomber Command was once more committed to the strategic bombardment of Germany. German oil plants had the first priority, but marshalling yards, ship-building yards, aircraft factories, etc, also figured in the directive. Berlin was to be attacked whenever con-

ditions were favourable. In all cases the targets were pin-point objectives, and in the weather prevailing over Germany at that season of the year, it is not surprising that they were very hard to find and identify. Some of the more highly trained and skilled crews occasionally achieved individual successes in low-level moonlight attacks on oil targets but the cumulative effects were negligible. Thus, by and large, precision bombing was virtually hopeless and, as this fact gradually became recognised, thoughts began to turn to the concept of 'area bombing' in which the force available on any one night was given as its target the centre of an industrial town where a considerable degree of scatter would still result in a large number of bombs doing heavy material damage.

Wherever the bombs may have fallen on Berlin in the raid of August 25/26, the first deliberate area attack was not mounted until after the *Luftwaffe's* indiscriminate bombing of Coventry on November 14/15, the date being December 16/17 and the target Mannheim. Code-named Operation *Abigail*, the raid was made in perfect moonlight conditions and opened by a force of fire-raising Wellingtons armed with incendiary bombs and flown by the most experienced crews available. Altogether, 134 aircraft took part, and 47 Wellingtons, 33 Whitleys, 18 Hampdens and four Blenheims claimed to have attacked Mannheim, crew reports unanimously suggesting that most of the bombs had fallen in the target area.

Among the aircraft which did not reach Mannheim was Whitley V P5109 of 10 Squadron; its starboard

engine failed completely within 60 miles of the target, forcing the pilot, Plt Off Brant, to abandon the mission and head for home. The Whitley rapidly lost height and, in an effort to lighten it, all rear turret ammunition was fired at searchlights over Holland from 3,000ft; and all front gun ammunition, the front and rear guns themselves, and all other moveable objects were jettisoned over the North Sea. By the time this was done the Whitley was only 1,500ft above the sea, but Brant gradually coaxed it to 2,500ft. On reaching the English coast the height again dropped to 2,000ft but Bircham Newton airfield was located and a safe landing made – with only seconds to spare, for just before touching down the port engine cut out also.

Within a week of this raid, and after further light attacks on Mannheim, a photo-reconnaissance Spitfire managed to photograph the city in daylight. From the mosaic it was clear that although 'considerable damage' had been done, the attack had been widely scattered, some of the fires having been started outside the target area, thus leading the following crews astray.

Italian cities figured in the target lists again in the closing months of 1940, small forces being despatched to attack industries in Milan and Turin on six nights during November and December. The 1,350-mile round trip with its double crossing of the Alps was always a big challenge to the bombers and on the night of November 5/6 weather conditions were so severe that only one of the 19 Whitleys which set out from England succeeded in reaching Italy. Plt Off H. H. J. Miller and his crew of 77 Squadron certainly found it a night to remember. On the outward journey lightning struck the aircraft and put the radio out of action. Then, over the Alps, thick clouds with ice and snow were encountered and the temperature fell to −20°C. The bombs were dropped from 8,000ft in cloud on ETA (Estimated Time of Arrival) over Turin and by the time the Alps had been re-crossed all members of the crew were frozen stiff. When the rear gunner asked permission to come forward from his lonely station in the tail to thaw out and to have something to eat, he found that he was so stiff that he could not get out of the turret, and when he tried to break a piece of chocolate it was frozen so hard that even banging it on the guns failed to shatter it. While crossing the North Sea the fuel ran out but the captain managed to ditch the Whitley four miles off the English coast near a naval minefield patrol boat and all the crew were rescued. The patrol boat had been at anchor on the outside of a coastal magnetic minefield which protected our convoys from enemy surface raiders as they moved between it and the coast, and if the Whitley crew had landed 200yds nearer the coast they would almost certainly have blown themselves up!

On September 3, 1940, the first anniversary of the outbreak of war, Winston Churchill, the Prime Minister, had written his famous minute to the War Cabinet in which he had stated: '. . . The Navy can lose us the War, but only the Air Force can win it. Therefore our supreme effort must be to gain overwhelming mastery in the air. The Fighters are our salvation but the Bombers alone can provide the means of victory. We must, therefore, develop the power to carry an ever-increasing volume of explosives to Germany, so as to pulverise the entire industry and scientific structure on which the war effort and economic life of the enemy depend, while holding him at arm's length from our Island. In no other way at present can we hope to overcome the immense military power of Germany . . .'

By the end of the year, Bomber Command was unable to make anything but pinpricks in the enemy's side and it knew that for a long time to come its efforts would have to continue to be conducted on the principle of trial and error. Even before the war the Air Staff had realised that if the bombers had to operate by night they would have difficulty in finding and attacking their targets by visual methods, though perhaps they did not fully appreciate the magnitude of the problem. For this reason, requirements had been issued for night bombing aids, but until the Battle of Britain was over all priorities had rightly been concentrated on air defence. However, by now the first radio aids to

Sting in the nose. Unusual view of the twin .303in Browning-armed Frazer-Nash nose turret of a Wellington IA or IC taken in September 1940. This type of nose turret remained standard on all subsequent operational bomber marks of the Wellington through to the final B.Mk X.

navigation were being developed by the back room 'boffins', and, of more immediate importance to Bomber Command, the first fruits of the pre-war second-generation big bomber projects were beginning to enter service. The first Short Stirling Is had reached 7 Squadron at RAF Leeming, Yorks, in August, and in the following month the first Avro Manchester Is and Handley Page Halifax Is had been delivered respectively to the nucleus of 207 Squadron at Boscombe Down, Wilts, and to 35 Squadron at Linton-on-Ouse, Yorks. None of the new heavies were to become operational until the New Year, and before then Bomber Command was to encounter what was to prove an ever-present difficulty in carrying out its strategic bombing campaign against Germany. What happened was that in December, after the area bombing raid on Mannheim, the Admiralty started clamouring for action against the U-boat bases at Lorient and Bordeaux as well as the construction yards in Germany, so that by the end of 1940 as big a weight of bombs was being aimed against naval targets as against all other types of targets combined. Indeed, it was not long before Churchill himself issued a directive giving absolute priority to the Battle of the Atlantic, with the results that will be described in Volume 2.

Camouflage Schemes

Introduction of camouflage and special markings.

When Bomber Command was formed in 1936 bomber aircraft were still placed in two categories – day bombers and night bombers. Only the single squadron of Boulton Paul Overstrands, No 101 at Bicester, defied any clear-cut categorisation, being considered as 'twin-engined fighting day and night bombers'. The Overstrand was something of a mixed-role type, being much heavier than the usual day bomber class but smaller and faster than the heavy night bombers that were its contemporaries. It was considered agile and well-armed enough to look after itself if intercepted in daylight. Day bombers and Overstrands in service were sprayed in Aluminium (silver) on fabric and wood, with polished natural metal plating over certain areas of the airframe, notably around engine cowlings.

Type A roundels using Bright Red (DTD 71 & 72), white (DTD 75 & 76) and Bright Blue (DTD 67 & 68) were used on the upper and lower wings and on the fuselage sides. In earlier years upper and lower wing roundels were of large size extending from approximately 1in inboard of the leading edge to 1in inboard of the trailing edge. However, by 1936 the ruling had been made that roundels were not to be painted over moving surfaces to avoid balance problems and to prevent paint from interfering with hinges and operating rods. Roundels were therefore painted on the fixed area, leaving a 1in gap between the outside ring of the roundel and the nearest movable part (such as a slat or aileron). In practice the amount of gap left between the roundel and the moving part depended on the size of roundel chosen for a particular aircraft type, and the positioning of the roundel spanwise. Type A roundel sizes were usually determined by selecting a convenient ring width, say 8in, and multiplying by the five ring widths in a red, white and blue roundel (8in x 5in = 40in). The overall size was usually chosen as being

Finishing the tail unit of a Harrow I at Handley Page's Radlett works in April 1937. The power-operated twin-gun rear turret is not fitted on this aircraft. Even without masking, the spray guns produced a comparatively sharp edge to the camouflage pattern. On some production lines, flexible masking mats were used when spraying the camouflage pattern.

the largest diameter to fit inside the fixed area of wing that was divisable by five, and which cleared the moving parts of the wing by not less than 1in.

The roundel sizes used for the various types of day bomber in service with Bomber Command in 1936 were as follows:

Aircraft type	Fuselage	Upper Wing	Lower Wing
Hawker Hart	25in	35in	55in
Hawker Hind	25in	35in	55in
Westland Wallace	25in	35in	40in
Fairey Gordon	25in	45in	45in
Boulton Paul Overstrand	35in	50in	50in

Fuselage serial numbers on all these types were 8in high. Underwing serials were in the following sizes:

Hawker Hart	30in
Hawker Hind	30in
Westland Wallace	30in
Fairey Gordon	30in
Boulton Paul Overstrand	45in

During 1936 the heavy night bombers in service were finished overall in Nivo (Night Invisible Varnish, Orfordness), which was a dull fir green. The Handley Page Heyford, Vickers Virginia and Fairey Hendon were all painted in Nivo. Type B roundels were used on fuselage sides and upper and lower wing tips. In the type B roundel, only Dull Blue (Stores ref DTD 33B/69 and 70) and Dull Red (stores ref DTD 33B/73 & 74) were used. Dull Blue was a very dark blue and Dull Red was a brick red-brown in shade – closer to brown than red. The proportions of the Type B roundel were determined by the Dull Red centre being 2/5ths of the overall roundel diameter. The approximate roundel sizes are given below for each of the main night bombers:

Aircraft Type	Fuselage	Upper Wing	Lower Wing
Handley Page Heyford	50in	60in	60in
Vickers Virginia	45in	85in	85in
Fairey Hendon	50in	60in	60in

The under wing serial letters and numerals were painted in white, and were approximately 60in high on Heyfords and Hendons and 84in high on Virginias.

During exercises these white serial numbers were often overwashed with green temporary distemper to render them less conspicuous. The serial number was also painted in black in 8in high letters and numerals on the rear fuselage and on the rudder.

Individual aircraft letters were usually painted in Flight colours – usually Dull Red for A Flight, yellow for B Flight and Dull Blue for C Flight. One night bomber unit, 500 Squadron, a Special Reserve cadre

squadron until early in 1936, carried the squadron number and aircraft letters in white on its Virginias.

Adoption of the Expansion Scheme and its emphasis on the re-equipment of the RAF squadrons with modern monoplanes brought great changes to the finish of Service aircraft. The simple division of colour schemes between the sombre Nivo-painted night flying bombers and the brightly-adorned day flying fighters, light bombers, army co-operation and transport aeroplanes was to be replaced by a new camouflage scheme to be used on the upper surfaces of all new operational monoplanes. The new camouflage scheme consisted of a disruptive pattern using two colours, Dark Earth, a fairly dark sandy brown, and Dark Green, a colour darker than Nivo, with a more brown bias. Each manufacturer prepared individual camouflage pattern schemes for his particular aircraft type, based on a guide scheme produced by the Air Ministry to suit particular aircraft layouts governed by overall wing spans. Six different basic patterns were provided for guidance to manufacturers evolving camouflage schemes for their aircraft: for single-engined fighters, trainers and other monoplanes, twin-engined monoplanes of all types under 70ft span, twin-engined monoplanes of all types over 70ft span, four-engined monoplanes, single-engined biplanes, and twin-engined biplanes. Naturally, these patterns only acted as a rough guide and manufacturers prepared their own camouflage pattern to suit the particular design features and contours of their aircraft. Obviously, individual cases, such as twin fins and rudders on some aircraft, and a single fin and rudder on others, required suitable pattern changes. The shape of fuselages and nacelles necessitated modification of the recommended patterns. The basic reason for adopting the new camouflage finish was to render the aircraft much less visible from above, either when dispersed on an aerodrome or when flying at low or medium heights.

When the new camouflage scheme was introduced on the upper surfaces of the new monoplanes going into production during 1936, the under surfaces were finished in two different forms: single-engined fighters remained unchanged in the inter-war years colour scheme of Aluminium, with black serial numbers and Type A roundels under the wings; all types of bombers from single-engined to multi-engined, had a new undersurface scheme of Night (black) overall with white serial letters and numerals under the wings.

The new camouflage scheme was always intended to be applied in two forms on the production lines – A-scheme and B-scheme. The B-scheme was the exact 'mirror' image of the A-scheme: the pattern which appeared, say, on the port side of the fuselage in the A-scheme would be applied to the starboard side of the fuselage in the B-scheme, and vice versa. Usually, the first aircraft of a particular production batch would be finished in A-scheme pattern and the second in B-scheme, and so on.

Plans were laid for the new camouflage schemes to be used in two forms – normal peacetime, with conspicuous national markings and squadron and aircraft identification, and war emergency markings, with inconspicuous dull identification markings.

The first new production aircraft to feature the new markings was the Handley Page Harrow. The first production Harrow I, K6933, was completed in November 1936 and was finished in Dark Earth and Dark Green on the upper surfaces, with overall Night on the under surfaces. Handley Page added their own interpretation of the new camouflage scheme by adding a wavy edge to the Night areas on the fuselage, wings, tailplane, nacelles and wheel spats.

The camouflage pattern prepared for the Harrow was based on the pattern guide for twin-engined monoplanes over 70ft span.

During 1936 and 1937 there was no immediate threat of war, and consequently the new camouflage scheme was introduced into the production lines with peacetime national markings. In order to make the Royal Air Force roundels conspicuous against the drab colours of Dark Earth and Dark Green they were outlined with an additional ring of yellow. This produced the now familiar Type A.1 roundel. As the Type A.1 roundel had seven ring widths it was usual for the manufacturer of a particular aircraft type to select roundel diameters that were divisible by seven in order to ease painting problems. Thus, a 49in roundel, say, would be selected for the fuselage position instead of a 4ft diameter roundel because the former contained seven ring widths of 7in each.

The Handley Page Harrow had fuselage Type A.1 roundels of 49in in diameter and the upper wing Type A.1 roundels were 63in in diameter. The serial number was carried under each wing, 48in high in white. The serial number was also carried on the rear fuselage and on the rudders in black in letters and numerals 8in high.

About the same time that the first Harrow was being prepared for its trials, K7034, the second Bristol Blenheim off the production line at Filton, was being completed. Like the Harrow this Blenheim, and subsequent Blenheims for the RAF bomber squadrons, was finished in Dark Earth and Dark Green to A and B scheme patterns based on the guide scheme for twin-engined monoplanes under 70ft span.

On the Blenheim Mk I at this period the fuselage Type A.1 roundels were 45.5in in diameter (6.5in ring widths) and the upper wing Type A.1 roundels were 66.5in in diameter (9.5in ring widths).

The under wing serial letters and numerals were initially 30in high, painted in white, but eventually the height of these was increased to 36in and set closer inboard. 8in high black serial letters and numerals were used on the rear fuselage position and on the rudder.

The first production-type Vickers Wellesley was

Blenheim Is of 114 Squadron in 1937. A and B scheme camouflage patterns can be seen on these aircraft, the Blenheim in the foreground having the A scheme. The walkway colour was grey. The wing roundels are positioned inboard at approximately the regulation $\frac{1}{3}$ of the half span/*Bristol Aeroplane Co*

completed towards the end of January 1937, and this was also painted in the new camouflage scheme. The unusual proportions of the Wellesley, with its wing span of 74ft 7in and length of 39ft 3in, combined with a single-engine, raised problems in the selection of a suitable pattern. An official guide pattern for such a large single-engined monoplane did not exist. Eventually it was decided to adopt the official pattern for twin-engined monoplanes under 70ft span, this being the most suitable because the fuselage was similar in size to an average twin-engined medium bomber. The prepared camouflage scheme was very similar in pattern to that used on the Bristol Blenheim.

The upper wing Type A.1 roundels used on the Wellesley were 49in in diameter and those on the fuselage were 35in in diameter. Under wing white serial letters and numerals were 36in high. The usual 8in high black serials were used on the rear fuselage and rudder.

Adding greatly to its purposeful appearance, full camouflage was also applied to the first production Whitley I, which was completed on the Baginton line in March 1937. Based generally on the official pattern for twin-engined monoplanes of over 70ft span, the pattern used on the Whitley was very similar to that used on the Harrow. The fuselage Type A.1 roundels were 49in in diameter but, unlike the Harrow, the Type A.1 roundels used on the wing upper surface were 105in in diameter, to match the very broad chord of the Whitley wing.

The white underwing serial letters and numerals were 45in high, and the usual 8in high black serials were painted at the rear fuselage position and on the rudders.

Another of the new bombers to leave the production

lines for the first time was K7558, the first production Fairey Battle, which was completed early in 1937. The camouflage pattern used on the Battle was based, because of its size, on the official pattern for twin-engined monoplanes of under 70ft span. The Type A.1 fuselage roundels were 35in in diameter, and the wing upper surface roundels were 42in in diameter, also Type A.1. The white underwing serial letters and numerals were 40in high. The fuselage and rudder serials were 8in high and painted in black.

Early in 1937 the new monoplane bombers were delivered to RAF squadrons to urgently replace the obsolete biplanes. The Harrow was the first to enter service, the first delivery being made to 214 Squadron on January 13. In service during 1937 and up to August 1938 Harrows had the squadron number and aircraft letters added to the basic camouflage scheme. At first in 214 Squadron these were painted in yellow, as were those of 75 Squadron, but later grey (33B/157) became commonly used for squadron numbers and individual aircraft letters. Harrows usually had the squadron number forward of the fuselage roundel, with the aircraft letter aft of the roundel and repeated on the sides of the nose. In some cases, where the number and aircraft letter either side of the roundel was painted in yellow, the forward aircraft letter was painted grey. In some cases the forward letters were painted in the flight

Vickers Wellesley interim medium bombers in 1937. The camouflage pattern can be seen to be similar to that used on the Blenheim and Battle. The roundels were set near the wing tips because of the high aspect ratio of the wing. If they had been positioned at the normal $\frac{1}{3}$ of the half span, with 1in clearance between leading edge and between the aileron gap, the roundel diameter would have been excessive.

colour, and in another case the aircraft letters, fore and aft, were painted white. This was a period of experimentation with different ways of presenting identification on the new camouflage finish, but eventually grey letters and numerals became universally used.

The Armstrong Whitworth Whitley I and Bristol Blenheim I were the next types to enter service, the Whitley joining 10 Squadron for the first time on March 9 and the first Blenheim reaching 114 Squadron on the following day.

10 Squadron's Whitleys at first carried only their individual aircraft letters aft of the roundels and on each side of the nose, initially in yellow and later in grey. Later, during 1937, the squadron number was carried forward of the fuselage roundel and the aircraft letter aft of the roundel, also in grey (33B/157). Some aircraft carried an additional aircraft letter on each side of the nose, painted in the flight colour.

The other newly-equipped Whitley squadrons carried their squadron numbers and aircraft letters in a similar manner.

The first squadron to receive Blenheims, No 114, and its station rivals, 139 Squadron, carried the squadron number aft of the fuselage roundels in Dull Red outlined in black. 114 Squadron carried its aircraft letters on the nose, on each side in white, whereas 139 appears to have painted its letters in the flight colours. 90 and 44 Squadrons also received Blenheim Is during 1937 and these carried the squadron number and aircraft letters in grey. Other squadrons followed suit in 1938. 61 Squadron had the squadron number and aircraft letters in yellow outlined in black. This squadron was unorthodox in carrying its aircraft letters on the outer engine cowlings.

A feature of some Blenheim squadrons during 1937 and early 1938 was the painting of the undercarriage fairings in the flight colour.

Fairey Battles were first delivered to RAF squadrons in May 1937 when deliveries were made to 63 Squadron. 63 Squadron's Battles had letters and numerals painted in yellow, but squadron number and aircraft letters were usually grey on most Battle squadrons.

Munich

In March, 1938, German troops marched into Austria and by the summer of that year the international situation worsened dramatically. War, which had at one time seemed remote, now seemed near and plans were put into effect to place the RAF on a war footing. Hitler was by now demanding that certain parts of Czechoslovakia should be given to Germany, and by September 1938 the Munich Crisis broke upon an anxious Europe. While Britain and France exerted pressure on the Czechs to accept the German ultimatum, the RAF made modifications to the camouflage schemes of its aircraft to render them less conspicuous in the air and on the ground. Another important consideration was security and in order to hide

the number of new squadrons being formed or re-equipped with new types, and to hide the identity of existing squadrons, a code letter system was introduced on aircraft in place of the squadron number. In this system two letters were used to denote a particular squadron in place of the number, and this was painted either forward or aft of the fuselage roundel with the aircraft letter on the other side of the roundel. The positioning of the squadron code letters was not subject to a strict ruling: in some cases the letters were placed, say, forward of the roundel on the port side and aft of the roundel on starboard. In others, they would be painted aft of the roundel on each side. The letters were authorised to be painted in 'grey paint, Stores ref 33B/157' (this is the same stores reference as Medium Sea Grey. It was presumably given the official name Medium Sea Grey when other greys, such as Dark Sea Grey, Extra Dark Sea Grey, Sky Grey, etc came into use.) The letters were to be 48in high, with 6in strokes. Smaller letters were, however, permitted where space on a fuselage did not allow letters of this height to be used. This somewhat loose ruling resulted in a wide variety of letter sizes and styles being used, not only on different aircraft types, but also on individual squadrons flying a similar type. The Whitleys of 51 and 58 Squadrons, for instance, had 48in high code letters,

Fairey Battles of 12 Squadron over their base at Bicester, Oxon, in May 1939. The aircraft are in the process of being converted to War Emergency markings to render them less conspicuous. The difference between the original Type A.1 and the converted Type B roundels is striking. The top aircraft has Type B fuselage and Type A.1 wing roundels. Some aircraft have aircraft letters, but the squadron code letters have not yet been applied.

whereas those used by 102 Squadron were 36in high. Blenheims, Battles and Hampdens were not deep enough in the fuselage to accommodate 48in high letters, and smaller sizes were used on these aircraft.

The most important aspects of the programme to make operational aeroplanes less conspicuous was the re-painting of day bombers, army co-operation aircraft and fighters still in their Aluminium-sprayed finish with a new camouflage scheme of Dark Earth and Dark Green, and the conversion of the Type A.1 roundels to the sombre Type B Dull Blue and Dull Red roundels.

As the Munich Crisis deepened it became necessary to hurriedly camouflage large numbers of bright Aluminium-coloured aeroplanes. Many Hinds still remained in service and War Emergency markings had to be applied to them as soon as possible, which meant over-painting with Dark Earth and Dark Green on the upper surfaces, applying Type B roundels and painting on grey code and aircraft letters. The under surfaces were usually left in their existing Aluminium (silver) finish.

At the time of the crisis at least two squadrons were flying Heyfords and 38 Squadron was still equipped with the Hendon. As these bombers were already painted in the dull Nivo night bomber scheme, with Type B roundels, it is probable that they were not repainted to the new camouflage requirements. All of these obsolete aircraft were about to be replaced by modern monoplanes at that time and there is no evidence to prove that any change to their existing finish was made. The Virginias of the Home Aircraft Depot at Henlow, however, did have their existing all-Dull Red paint replaced by Dark Earth and Dark Green.

The most important single item in the repainting programme related to the conversion of Type A.1 roundels into Type B on the new types of bombers, fighters and army co-operation monoplanes which had recently come into service. Conversion of Type A.1 roundels into Type B was usually carried out by using the existing Dull Blue ring as a guide. The centre Dull Red spot was enlarged to two-fifths of the Dull Blue ring diameter, and the Dull Blue areas then extended up to the Dull Red centre. The yellow outer ring was then over-painted with the respective Dark Earth or Dark Green pattern up to the Dull Blue ring. This, of course, resulted in all the national markings being reduced in size. In the following table Type B roundel sizes after conversion from Type A.1 are given for the new monoplane bombers:

Type	Fuselage		Wing upper surface	
	Dull Blue dia	Dull Red dia	Dull Blue dia	Dull Red dia
Harrow	35in	14in	45in	18in
Whitley	35in	14in	75in	30in
Hampden	25in	10in	45in	18in
Blenheim	32.5in	13in	47.5in	19in
Battle	25in	10in	30in	12in
Wellesley	25in	10in	35in	14in
Wellington	35in	14in	45in	18in

While conversion of existing Service aircraft was taking place at operational bomber stations, maintenance units and aircraft storage units, the manufacturing firms prepared new camouflage drawings in order to introduce the War Emergency markings onto the production lines. Type B roundels introduced on production aircraft usually differed in size from those converted in the RAF, often reverting to the original Type A.1 roundel size. Roundels on production bombers after the change to Type B from the end of 1938 until late 1939 are given in the table below:

Type	Fuselage		Wing upper surface	
	Dull Blue dia	Dull Red dia	Dull Blue dia	Dull Red dia
Whitley	50in	20in	84in	34in
Hampden	35in	14in	64in	26in
Blenheim	35in	14in	66.5in	26.5in
Battle	42in	17in	42in	17in
Wellington	35in	14in	63in	25.2in

The Harrow and Wellesley, although still in service, were by this time no longer in production. By the time the Munich Crisis arose the Hampden had replaced the Harrow on the Handley Page production line and the Wellington had replaced the Wellesley on the Vickers line at Brooklands. Type B roundels on these types of aircraft were, therefore, all conversions from Type A.1.

The under surfaces of all types of the new monoplane bombers were usually left unchanged – Night overall, with large white serial letters and numerals. If war had come during that autumn of 1938 it is probable that these conspicuous markings would have been painted out with additional Night paint.

Early in 1939, after the immediate crisis had passed and before the final crisis plunged the world into war, Type A roundels were added to the bomber under surfaces, outboard of the serial letters and numerals.

During this period, from the autumn of 1938 and early in 1939, many markings anomalies were to be

seen on airfields up and down the country. New production bombers were being delivered to squadrons, many still with Type A.1 roundels awaiting conversion. Generally, Type B roundels had, early in 1939, only just started to be introduced onto the production lines. It was not uncommon at this time to see aircraft flying with Type A.1 roundels and grey code and aircraft letters. In some cases, especially during roundel conversion painting interrupted for flying training, bombers could be seen with Type A.1 roundels on the upper wings and Type A or B roundels on the fuselage sides. In other cases, the reverse would apply. General attention, though, was paid to painting the operational squadron aircraft in accordance to the required markings standards, with most of the anomalies appearing on reserve and non-operational aircraft.

The full requirement relating to the camouflage and markings of RAF aircraft of all types during the change to War Emergency markings was outlined in Air Ministry Order 154/39, amended by AMO 298/39 issued on April 27, 1939. These orders confirmed the use of Type B roundels on upper wings and fuselage sides, Type A roundels under wing tips and Grey (Stores ref 33B/157) code letters and aircraft letter either side of the fuselage roundels when used on bombers. A concession to peacetime was the permitted painting of squadron badges onto aircraft, provided that these could be easily removed without trace at short notice. On bombers the central design motif of the badge was usually painted within the standard 'grenade' symbol and carried on the nose or tail unit. Examples of this practice were 9 Squadron's green bat motif painted on the noses of its Wellingtons, 58 Squadron's owl adorning the noses of its Whitley IIIs and the black swan badge carried on the fins of 103 Squadron's Battles.

Hampden I of 44 Squadron pre-war. The variation in code and aircraft letter size is noteworthy. The light tone of the letters and outer ring of the roundel and the dark centre spot are due to the the type of film used.

The months following the Munich Crisis saw a general bringing into line of aircraft markings with the official directives. This involved the RAF in a massive programme of conversion of roundels and the painting of code and aircraft letters in place of the existing squadron number, which necessitated the expenditure of many man hours. The introduction of the revised markings on the production lines of various aircraft factories gradually reduced the number of man hours required within the RAF units and also reduced the anomalies. As has always been the case throughout the history of aircraft markings, this period was one during which it was possible to record odd anomalies in markings – particularly so when vast numbers of aircraft were in the process of being converted and having paint work touched up, and yet at the same period were engaged on intensive flying training. It was always possible to record examples of aircraft having, say, Type B roundels surrounded by an outer ring of yellow, simply because the painters had not, as yet, over-painted the old existing yellow ring of the original Type A.1 roundel with the respective camouflage colours.

It is true to say that such deviations, however temporary, have always attracted attention from enthusiasts, who tend to ignore the authorised markings in favour of the unusual. Although this is a purely natural reaction it would be wrong to suggest that the official directives on markings were ignored. In fact the vast majority of aircraft were painted strictly in accordance with laid-down directives appertaining at that time. Signals were sent by the Air Ministry to both RAF units concerned and to the Resident Technical Officers (the RTOs, the link-men between the Ministry and the industry, who resided at each aircraft factory – normally close to the design and technical personnel). These signals, and other similar means of communication, were sent whenever changes were required to be made to camouflage and markings schemes – some to be acted upon immediately, while others were to be introduced as soon as convenient without interrupting flying or production. Thus both

the RAF and the aircraft industry acted jointly on markings changes, as can often be confirmed from a check on the dates when markings were changed in RAF squadrons and the dates quoted on the official colour scheme drawings prepared by various companies. It is often suggested that the RAF and the industry worked independently with regard to camouflage schemes, but this is not so. Part of the production contract was that up-to-date camouflage scheme drawings had to be prepared for use with the particular aircraft type. From these drawings numbers of prints were made and squadrons using the aircraft in question were ordered to work to these drawings when re-painting, or any other alteration was being made to the aircraft's paint finish. Thus the RAF and the industry worked to the same basic drawings, but of course in the heat of the moment, touching up paint schemes after repair and similar activities, there were occasions when the camouflage patterns were hurriedly resprayed without reference to the drawings.

Even if all those engaged in aviation at that time did work to the official directives and authorised drawings this did not mean that there was strict uniformity. The overall basic camouflage scheme for bombers, Dark Green and Dark Earth upper surfaces, with Night undersides, was universally used and the upper surface patterns were similar for the various size classes. Code and aircraft letters were universally painted in grey (33B/157), and the position of serial numbers was similar on most types. But within these rules lay a variety of individual styles which prevented uniformity in detail. Code letter sizes varied considerably from one aircraft type to another. Some squadrons painted the two squadron identification code letters forward of the roundel on both sides of the fuselage, some aft on both sides, while others followed the more correct practice of having the letters forward of the roundel on one side and aft on the opposite side. The shade of the grey used for the code letters also depended on how well the paint was mixed before application, and some examples were probably more blue, or more brown, than the true colour. Code and aircraft letters also varied in style according to the whim of the particular squadron: some used 'square' lettering, whilst others used 'rounded' letters. The thickness of the letters varied from squadron to squadron, and in at least the case of 63 Squadron's Battles at the time of the Munich Crisis letters of varying thickness were used, producing a somewhat oriental style!

No further changes were made to camouflage up to the outbreak of World War II.

War
On the outbreak of the war on September 3, 1939, the only alteration made to existing camouflage schemes was that all code letters used by squadrons during

Top left: Wellington I, L4304, of 148 Squadron, pre-war. The use of two aircraft letters on one aircraft was also common to 9 Squadron. The reason for this is not known, but the aircraft may have been flown by two separate crews when insufficient aircraft were available.

Centre left: Whitley IV K9026 of 10 Squadron in 1939 before the outbreak of war. This aircraft was delivered with Type A.1 roundels and is seen in the partially converted stage. The wing roundels are still Type A.1.

Left: Wellington Is during the Air Defence Exercises held in August 1939. These aircraft are wearing the cross markings of 'Westland', which were painted over the existing Type B roundels in temporary washable white distemper. The photograph gives an excellent example of A and B scheme mirror image camouflage patterns./*Flight International*

Continued on page 137

COLOUR SECTION

1 Fairey Hendon II K5087 of 38 Squadron, based at Marham during 1937. The Hendon was the first monoplane bomber to enter service with the Royal Air Force. Although originally intended to become the standard replacement night bomber for the Vickers Virginia, the Hendon only fully equipped one squadron. One flight of 38 Squadron did, however, become the nucleus of a new squadron, 115, which shortly afterwards was armed with Harrows. The Fairey Hendon was dimensionally similar to the Avro Lancaster, having a wing span of 101ft 6in and a length of 69ft 7in.

2 Handley Page Harrow K6962 of 115 Squadron, based at Marham, late 1937. The Harrow was the first production aircraft for the RAF to be painted in the new upper surface camouflage scheme of Dark Green and Dark Earth. Under surfaces were Night. The Dull Red, white and Dull Blue roundels were outlined with an additional ring of Yellow to make them conspicuous during peacetime. The Dull Red letter 'M' probably indicates that this aircraft belonged to 'A' Flight.

3 Two Bristol Blenheim IV day bombers of 101 Squadron, based at Oakington, Cambs. These two Blenheims are painted in the typical day bomber markings of mid-1940. The upper surface colours were Dark Green and Dark Earth, with Sky overall on the under surfaces. The squadron code and aircraft letters were in Medium Sea Grey. The illustration shows variations in markings common in this period: SR-Y, T1825, has standard type A.1 fuselage roundels and wide fin stripes. The area of Sky paint is extended along the fuselage sides in an irregular line up to the tailplane. It is probable that the Sky paint was sprayed over the original delivery scheme of Night (black) by the squadron. SR-C, N6181, has a narrow yellow outline to the original type A roundel and narrow fin stripes. The Sky under surfaces are neatly sprayed, and it is probable that this Blenheim was delivered with type A fuselage roundels and Sky under surfaces earlier in 1940. The narrow yellow outline to the roundels and fin stripes were added to aircraft by the squadron.

4 Armstrong-Whitworth Whitley V N1372 of 77 Squadron, based at Driffield, April 1940. N1372 was probably delivered with Type B fuselage roundels, but these were modified, by an order issued on November 21, 1939, to Type A. Many Driffield Whitleys have been shown with fuselage roundels of the style illustrated. It is not known whether these roundels were a deliberate attempt to reduce the conspicuousness of the roundel or were photographed during a period when they were being converted to a smaller Type A.

5 Whitley V N1463 of 58 Squadron, showing the yellow outer ring on the fuselage roundel and fin stripes introduced after May 1, 1940.

6 Whitley V Z6625 of 78 Squadron, showing Special Night (RDM2) finish extended up the fuselage sides after September 4, 1940. The roundel white ring has been painted over with Medium Sea Grey, as used on the code letters.

7 Vickers Virginia X K2675 of 58 Squadron painted overall in Nivo. The Type B roundels were painted in Dull Blue and Dull Red.

8 Fairey Gordon of 207 Squadron. By 1936 the rudder stripes had been removed.

9 Boulton Paul Overstrand K4553 of 101 Squadron, based at Bicester.
(The day bombers had their national markings painted in Bright Red, white and Bright Blue.)

10 Hawker Hind L7188 of 103 Squadron, based at Usworth, late 1938. It is probable that at about this time the squadron's aircraft were repainted on the upper surfaces in Dark Green and Dark Earth, with Type B roundels. Also at about this time Fairey Battles began to replace the squadron's Hinds.

11 Westland Wallace K3908 of 504 (County of Nottingham) Squadron.

12 Handley Page Heyford K4024 of 10 Squadron. Like the Virginia this aircraft is typical of heavy night bombers of 1936 period. The aircraft carries 'A' Flight markings in Dull Red.

13 Handley Page Harrow II K7009 of 214 Squadron based at Feltwell, Norfolk, during early 1938. 214 Squadron was the first to be equipped with Harrows.

14 Bristol Blenheim I K7170 of 61 Squadron, May 1938.

15 Fairey Battle I K7602 of 52 Squadron based at Upwood, Hunts, during early 1938.

16 Armstrong-Whitworth Whitley I K7185 of 10 Squadron. The Squadron became the first to receive Whitleys, which replaced Heyfords from March 9, 1937, onwards.

17 Vickers-Armstrongs Wellesley K8526 of 35 Squadron, based at Worthy Down, Hants, from July 1937.

18 Bristol Blenheim I L1113 of 62 Squadron. The grey used for painting squadron numbers, code or aircraft letters was ordered to be Stores Ref 33B/157. This is the same reference number as Medium Sea Grey.

19 Fairey Battle I L4958 of 63 Squadron, based at Upwood, Hunts. The aircraft is shown in the markings of late 1938 and up to the outbreak of war in September 1939.

20 Bristol Blenheim I L7059 of 90 Squadron, based at Bicester. The markings are those of late 1938 and up to the outbreak of war.

21 Armstrong-Whitworth Whitley III K8374 of 58 Squadron as it appeared in May 1939.

22 Vickers-Armstrongs Wellington I L4345 of 214 Squadron wearing the markings of 'Westland' during the Air Defence Exercises in August, 1939. The white cross was painted over the Type B roundels.
(The lighter outer ring around Type B roundels was the result of camouflage paint being applied over the yellow outer ring of the original Type A.1 roundels. It was usual for the Dull Blue ring to be extended inwards and the Dull Red centre extended outwards, with the red ring two-fifths of the diameter of the blue ring.)

23 Handley Page Hampden I L4194 of 185 Squadron, June 1939. The markings are interesting in that the code and aircraft letters have been painted over the yellow outer ring of the fuselage roundel in preparation for the conversion of the roundel to Type B. After conversion the letters would be in the correct position. The aircraft was delivered with Type A.1 roundels.

24 Vickers Wellington IA R3000 of 9 Squadron, showing the Type A fuselage roundel which replaced the Type B by order after November 21, 1939.

25 Bristol Blenheim IV L8756 of 139 Squadron, showing Sky overall on the under surfaces introduced at the end of 1939 on Blenheim day bombers.

26 Fairey Battle I K9330 of 226 Squadron, based in France. January 1940.

27 Handley Page Hampden I P1333 of 49 Squadron, in June 1940.

28 Vickers-Armstrongs Wellington IA P9206 of 75 Squadron in June 1940. Fin stripes and a yellow outer ring added to the fuselage roundel were painted on all RAF aircraft after the issue to units of signal X.485 on May 1, 1940.

29 Vickers-Armstrongs Wellington IC T2470 of 214 Squadron. The RDM2 Special Night paint used on all under surfaces was extended to cover approx $\frac{3}{4}$ of the fuselage sides and over the fin and rudder by an order issued on September 4, 1940. The wavy top line was unauthorised and led to controversy and an eventual order to make the top line straight. In some cases the wavy line adopted was much exaggerated and grotesque. When the Special Night paint was extended up the fuselage sides, the serial was repainted in Dull Red. Later in 1940 some squadrons over-painted the white, and in some cases the yellow, parts of the national markings to make them less conspicuous.

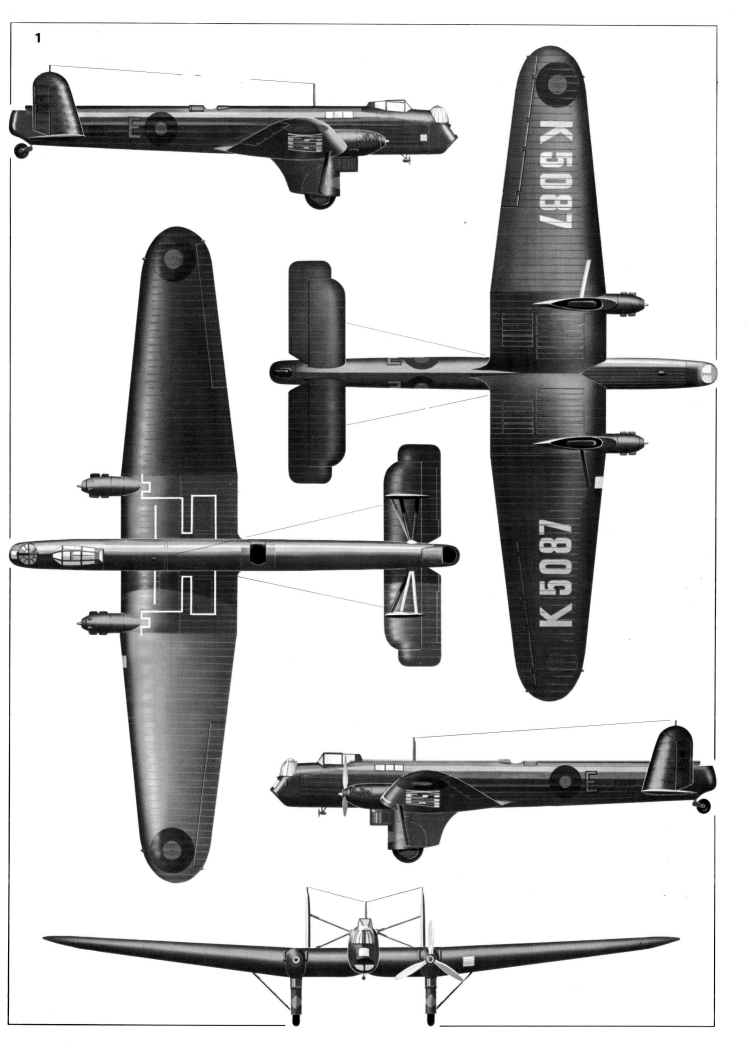

1

2

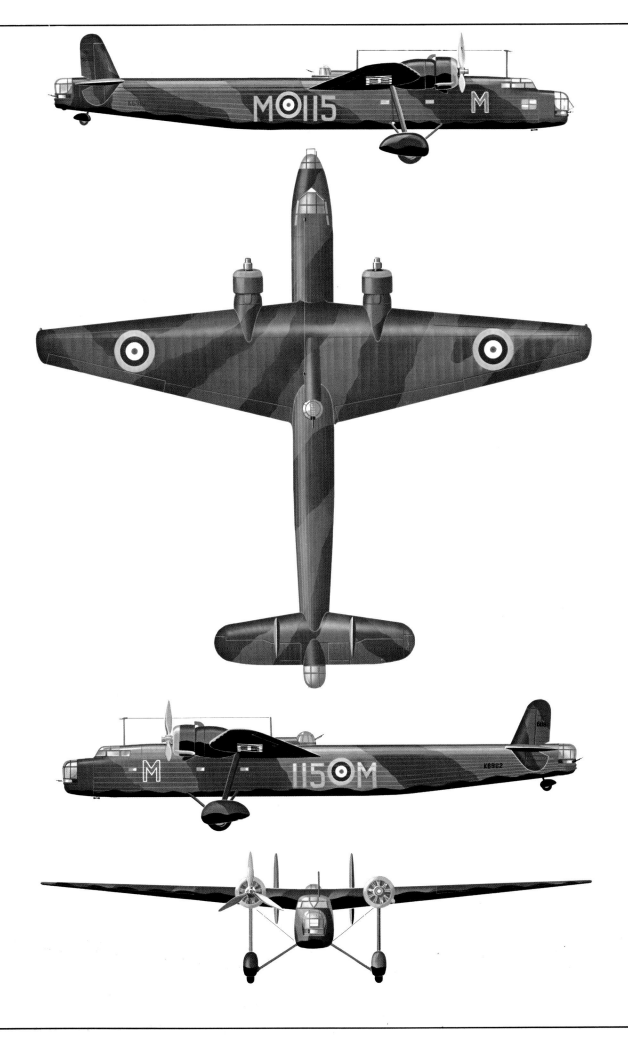

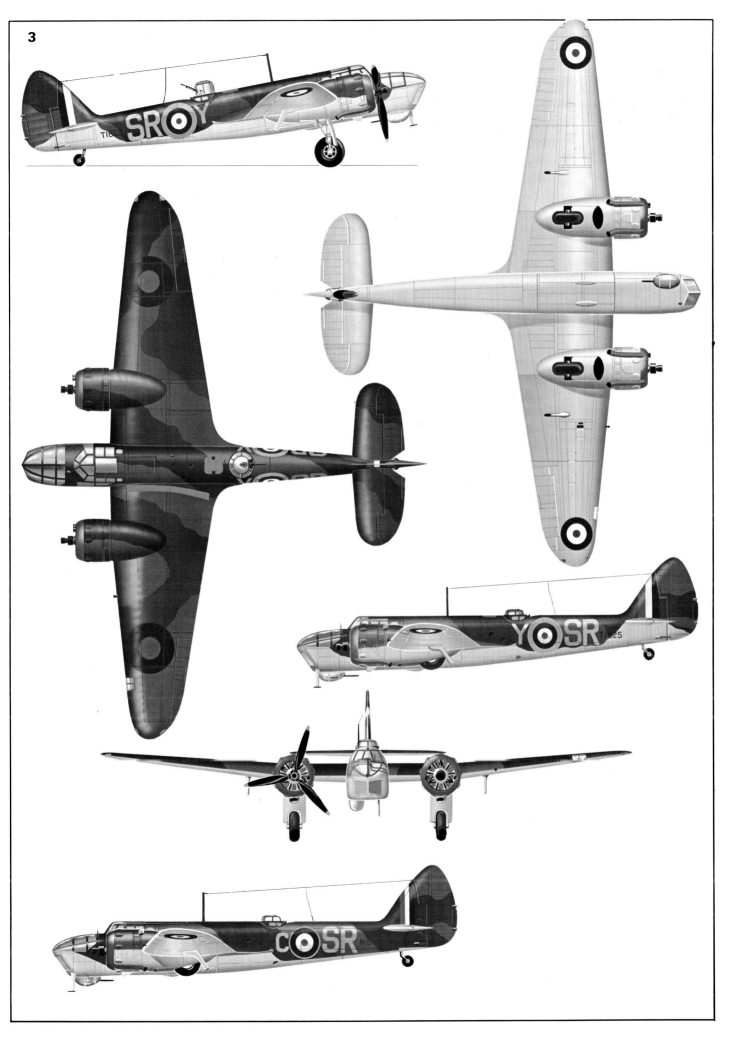

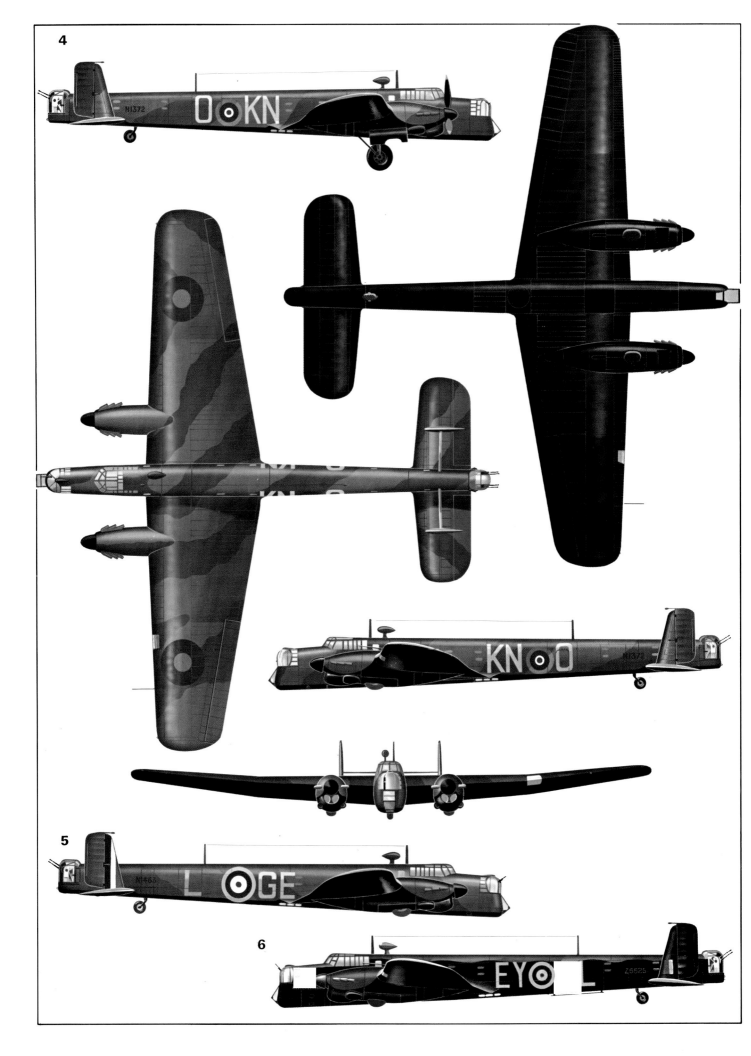

4

5

6

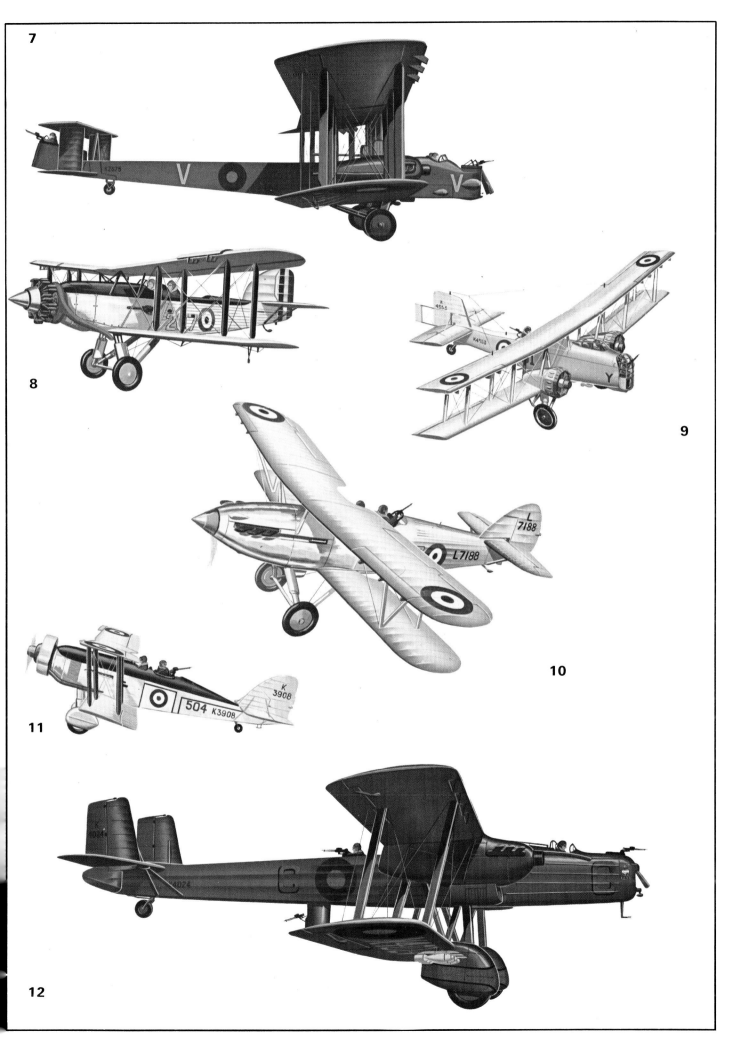

7

8

9

10

11

12

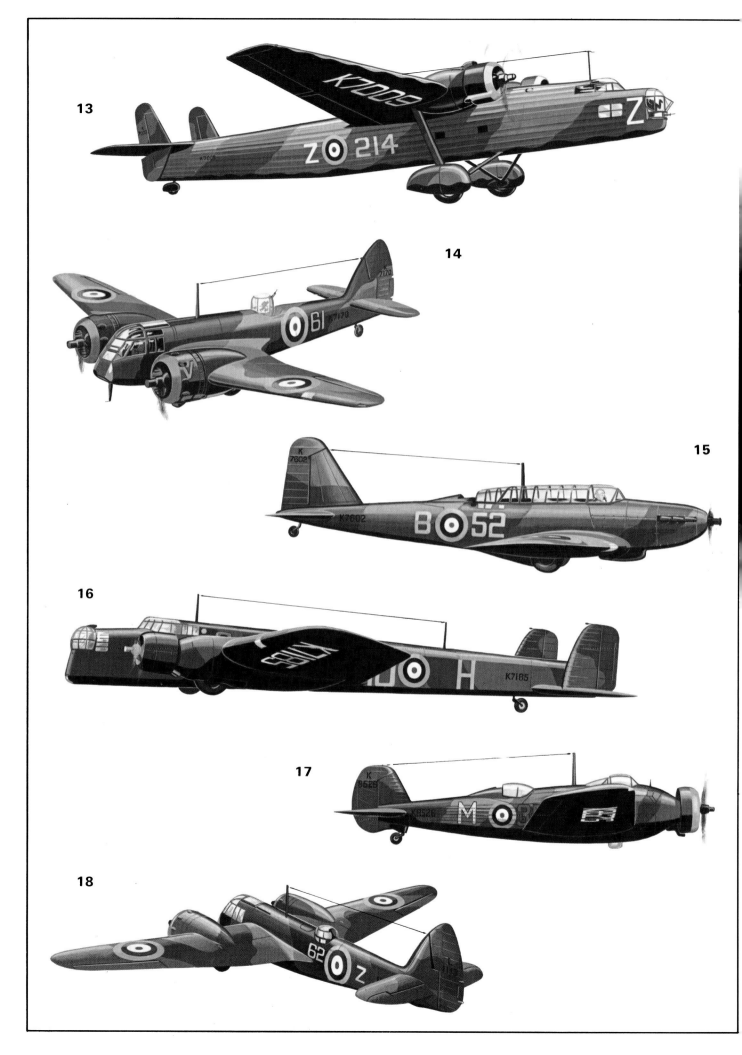

13

14

15

16

17

18

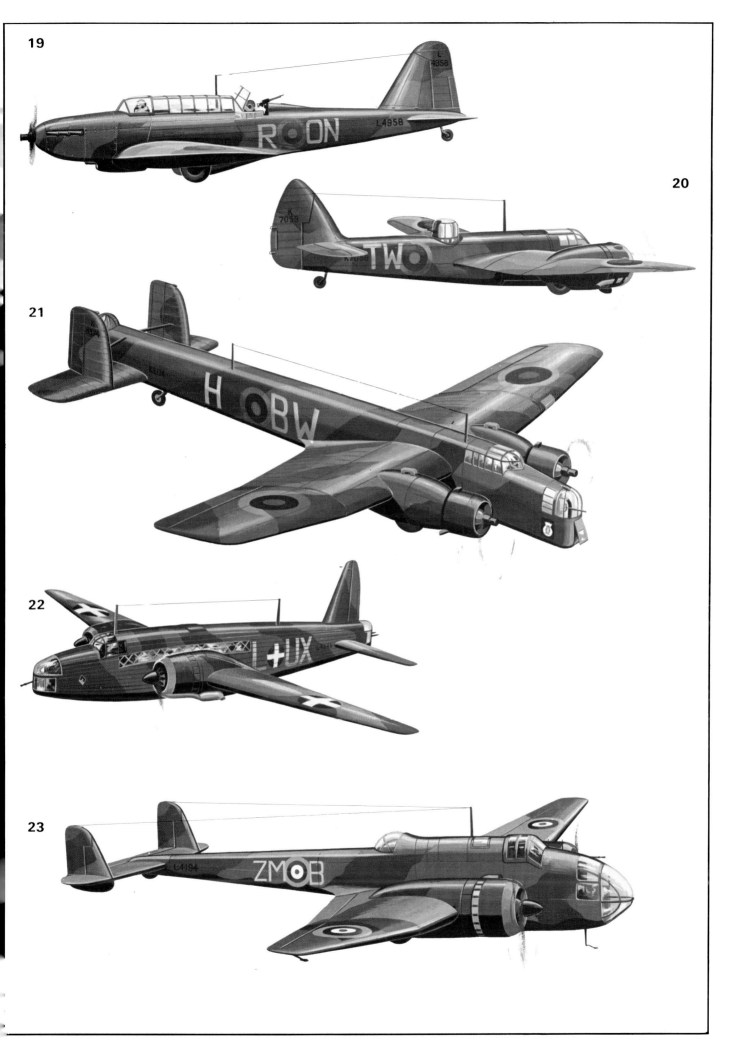

19

20

21

22

23

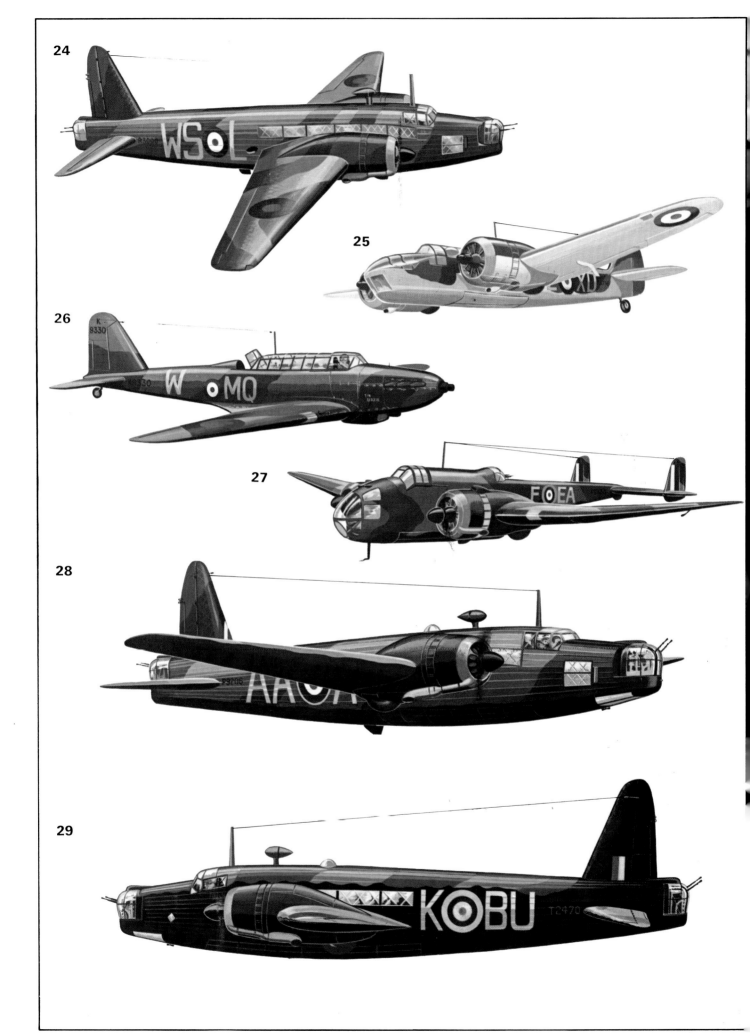

24

25

26

27

28

29

peacetime were changed. This necessitated squadrons painting out all existing squadron codes and repainting the new letters. This meant considerable touching up of the existing Dark Green and Dark Earth areas on the fuselage.

The only other alteration that may have been carried out to some aircraft was the painting out of serial numbers, particularly under the wings. The official directive on these was somewhat ambiguous. Officially, during peacetime they had been required to be white under the Night-painted under surfaces and in Night in 8in high letters and numerals at the rear of the fuselage. As war approached it became usual for the white under wing serials to be painted out in Night, although this was not officially confirmed as required to be done until later during 1939, after the outbreak of war. Squadrons, for their own protection and peace of mind, had generally painted these out long before the official directive, the official requirement merely putting on record what had become accepted practice. The rear fuselage serial numbers were usually left in the position as painted on during completion at the factory, but there were cases when these were painted out in the basic camouflage colours.

On May 22, 1939, two Wellington bombers at the Air Fighting Development Unit, then at Northolt, carried out trials of new anti-searchlight camouflage schemes, which were to lead to changes in the under surface finish, with much resulting anguish during usage. One of these aircraft was finished in the normal Dark Green/Dark Earth upper surface finish, with overall Night under surfaces. The second Wellington was painted Night overall for the initial comparison trials. At the time it was thought that extreme mattness of surface finish, of the darkest possible shade, was the ultimate goal in defeating searchlight pick-up – a logical notion that was to persist for many years. To achieve this aim a new paint was developed to produce a sooty, velvety surface finish which had complete mattness, without the sheen associated with existing dopes and pigmented varnishes.

At this time the standard paint finish on all camouflaged aircraft was known as Type M, which was regarded as a matt finish, but which still had a certain amount of surface sheen – far more in fact than is generally realised. The new under surface black paint for bombers was known by two official names, RDM2 or Special Night, and it was made from a number of substances (several changed during its development) including black-pigmented Benzyl or Ethyl cellulose and monolite Fast Black BS powder. Johnson's photographic black powder was also used during development trials.

One of the two Wellingtons was given an overall coating of RDM2 and flown on night trials. The paint on an aircraft gave a very rough, sooty surface finish that was only just stable when dry and which rubbed off a black surface deposit when touched. The night

trials suggested that application of the paint would be advantageous to night flying aircraft in avoiding detection from searchlights and a decision was made to provisionally adopt the new paint, pending the success of further trials to be carried out. To carry out more representative tests six aircraft from 6 Group, Bomber Command – three Blenheims and three Whitleys at Watton, Norfolk – were selected to be painted with RDM2 on their under surfaces, these trials commencing on or around August 15, 1939.

The progress of these trials seemed to confirm earlier promising results and on September 25, with Bomber Command now at war, 1,000 gallons of RDM2 Special Night dope was sent to 3 MU in preparation for the official authorisation from the Air Ministry for Bomber Command to use the new under surface finish. There was as yet little evidence of the difficulties that were to be encountered with the general use of the paint, nor of the lack of effectiveness of this new finish in countering searchlight illumination. The only small hint of problems to come lay in the difficulty in obtaining sufficient adhesive quality in the paint when applied to the undercoat. The standard Night paint was found to be the most satisfactory undercoat, a fortuitous discovery in view of the numbers of bombers with Night under surface finish that would eventually have to be overpainted with Special Night. The final decision to repaint all night flying aircraft in Bomber Command with RDM2 was made, and the order given, in January 1940.

The first months of the war saw little change in markings from peacetime, the change of code letters allotted to squadrons being the only major item. The upper surface finish consisted of the usual patterns of Dark Green and Dark Earth, with Night under surfaces. Code and aircraft letters were in grey (33B/157: at some stage, probably before the outbreak of war, this grey was given the official title of Medium Sea Grey. Its official title became more commonly used as the months passed and it was to become one of the most widely used paint colours in the RAF.) Type B roundels were painted on fuselage sides and on the upper wing surfaces. Bombers operating by day carried Type A under wing roundels, with the proviso that the white rings of these roundels should be painted out if the aircraft operated by night – which was accepted as meaning conversion of these roundels to Type B. The only bomber in squadron service which was classed as a night bomber when war broke out was the Whitley, and this class of aircraft was excluded from carrying under wing roundels. Some Whitleys had been delivered to the squadrons from factories and MUs with white serials and Type A roundels under the wings. These were generally over-painted with Night, but there were some cases when the roundels were retained but converted to Type B. 8in high Night-painted serials were painted on the rear fuselage, but some Blenheims and Battles operating in France had these painted over.

These markings continued in use until a tragic identification error caused a change in roundel type. It was obvious that under some conditions the existing markings were insufficiently conspicuous, and the hurried identification of a target could be faulty. On October 30 a telegram, A 949/39, was sent to all commands ordering Type A (red, white and blue) roundels to be painted on the upper surfaces of wings. This was followed by further telegrams, A 726/39 sent on November 5, and A 345/39 sent on November 10, reiterating that all RAF aircraft, except fighters and night bombers, were to carry Type A roundels under the wings.

The telegram of October 30 seems to have caused considerable confusion in the squadrons of Bomber and Fighter Command because the directive was evidently only intended to apply to general reconnaissance aircraft. It is not known if Type A roundels were ever applied to the upper wings of bombers. There is little photographic evidence to confirm that they were ever used on bombers or fighters, but they certainly were used on general reconnaissance aircraft, including Ansons, Hudsons and Sunderlands. It is certain that very few bombers, if any, had their Type B upper surface roundels converted to Type A. It is evident that it was intended at this time to make the fuselage roundels of all aircraft more conspicuous by converting the existing roundel to Type A by adding a ring of White.

All the confusion over roundels at this period was clarified by the issue of an amendment to Air Ministry Order No 154 on November 21, 1939, which again laid down rules for the markings to be carried by the various aircraft classes. Confirmation was given that only general reconnaissance aircraft were to have Type A upper wing roundels, but that all classes would have Type A fuselage roundels. Type A under wing roundels would be carried by all aircraft except night bombers and fighters.

An interesting entry in the amendment to AMO No 154 was that 'A very pale green surface (Sky Type S) is being applied to the under surface of Blenheims'. This is the first ever reference to the official use of Sky on the under surfaces of operational RAF aircraft, but its general adoption for use on the under surfaces of day flying aircraft was delayed until June 6, 1940.

Sky was evolved during trials with the Heston Flight, Wg Cdr Cotton's special unit undertaking photographic reconnaissance missions over enemy territory. In the late autumn of 1939 a Blenheim IV was sent from Wyton to Heston to undergo an extensive programme to improve its speed performance. This involved sealing all unnecessary cracks and applying a new surface finish to replace the existing Type M matt finish. This new finish used a more refined undercoat, involved much smoothing down with 'wet and dry' papers and the application of new, more refined camouflaged top coat paints. In addition to the new top coat paints to replace the earlier Type M finish paints, albeit still using the colours Dark Green and Dark Earth, a new under surface colour was evolved to provide camouflage up to medium heights against an average sky background. Letters sent to and from the Heston Flight refer to the new colour in descriptive terms because at that time an official title had not been given to the colour. A letter of November 18, quotes '. . . the under surfaces had been painted duck egg green, termed Camotint, which is said to render the aeroplane practically invisible at heights of 10,000ft or above'. Another, dated December 19, quotes '. . . it is noted that new dopes matching the standard camouflage colours, also a duck egg green, giving a smooth finish and without gloss are being supplied for trial at Heston.'

The new finish system, involving an improved undercoat, smoothing down surfaces and filled cracks and the new top coat refined paints, was given the official title of Type S. (Type S indicated the new smooth finish to differentiate it from the existing Type M matt finish). The new top coat colours supplied by the RAE for further trials initially had the titles Dark Green Type S, Dark Earth Type S and Sky Type S (the new official name for the 'duck egg green' shade), to differentiate them from the existing Type M, coarser versions of Dark Green and Dark Earth. Because Sky and the Type S system were introduced at one and the same time, both during the original trials, and when the two were authorised for general use on many classes of aircraft from June 6, 1940, the colour became referred to as Sky Type S, and even today it is still quoted as such. The suffix 'Type S' is however quite meaningless and is just one example of how a name can remain fixed in the popular imagination. Reference is never made to Dark Green Type S or Dark Earth Type S, yet these designations were used on camouflage and markings drawings when the Type S system was first introduced. The suffix 'Type S' was eventually dropped from the paint names, but continued to be used in popular parlance only with the colour Sky. Dark Green and Dark Earth were already well known when the Type S system was introduced, but Sky was a new colour introduced at the same time as the new finish system – therefore the two have become linked in the public mind and old habits are often impossible to break.

The same applies to the names given to Sky: there is no doubt that the popular name 'duck egg green' was the term by which the new colour was known when it was first used by the Heston Flight and No 2 Camouflage Unit at Heston. It was descriptive of the colour and it is

Left: An early production Whitley V showing the standard of markings applied on the factory production lines just before the outbreak of war. In war service the white serials were painted out with Night paint. The underwing roundels were usually painted out, but in some cases they were converted to Type B. The official directive stipulated that night bombers would not carry roundels under the wings.

by this name, for want of an official title at that time, that the colour is mentioned in correspondence. The official title, Sky, was most probably given to the colour by the RAE at Farnborough, but to those handling the tins and using the paint it remained 'duck egg green'. The situation became further confused when another descriptive name 'duck egg blue', began to be used widely in reference to Sky. Why the term 'duck egg blue' should have been used in preference to 'duck egg green' is obscure because the true shade was a pale greyish yellow-green. When Sky became authorised for general use on aircraft under surfaces there was considerable home-mixing of the colour, due to shortages of the true manufactured paint, and some of these attempts to produce the colour varied from pale conventional greens to pale blues. Possibly the term 'duck egg blue' became used on those units who had produced a more blue version of the colour.

The result of the use of these descriptive terms in place of the true name has been to give the impression that there were at least three different official paint shades, and many publications have, over the years, referred to 'duck egg green', 'duck egg blue', Sky Type S and Sky as being separate shades or official titles. Quotations from official correspondence and documents help to clarify the situation. DTD Spec 83 refers to the undersides of Blenheim bombers as 'a very pale green, Sky Type S'. DTD Spec 83A states that the under surfaces of certain classes or aircraft are 'duck egg blue'. An Admiralty supplement to these documents quotes . . . 'In order to clarify the position of the colour of under surfaces with this order and the camouflage drawings which will shortly be issued, it should be noted that duck egg blue and Sky Type "S" are one and the same colour.'

In official correspondence of November 14, 1940, the following is stated: 'The present under surface colour scheme of duck egg blue (standard "Sky") was intended for use only at moderate altitudes, and was originally used by Wg Cdr Cotton for experimental work at Heston, where it was found to be a decided improvement on the Aluminium then in use. This differs from the colour selected from the tests at the RAE for the same purpose and known as "Sky Blue" in that the former has a decided green tint and reflects less light.' Sky Blue, mentioned in this letter, was one of the standard colours listed in the official colour charts, and was similar in shade to the German colour *Hellblau* 65. It was developed before the outbreak of the war, and although tested for use on fighter and day bomber under surfaces, was never officially adopted for this purpose on land-based aircraft. Sky was more successful as an under surface colour because it was duller and less reflective.

The work at Heston on improving the surface finish of Blenheims resulted in a speed increase of 10-13mph, and the application of Sky to the under surfaces of the

test aircraft was so obviously successful that the decision to repaint Blenheim under surfaces with the new colour was announced in the amendment to AMO No 154, as mentioned earlier, before completion of all the tests. Blenheim bombers both at home and in France were repainted on their under surfaces from the end of 1939 and during the beginning of 1940. It is not known if all Blenheims were repainted or whether some were retained with Night finish for night operations. Although Sky was applied to Blenheims in France the Battles appear to have been left with Night undersides. Possibly the lower performance of the Fairey Battle rendered the aircraft too vulnerable for day operations and it was the intention to only use the type at night – but such intentions were quickly overruled by the desperate military situation in France after the German invasion.

In January 1940 it was decided to universally adopt RDM2 Special Night as the under surface colour for night bombers, without roundels. Day bombers painted with Night under surfaces had roundels, but the white ring was to be painted out if the aircraft was used at night.

On May 1, 1940, a major change took place in national markings. Signal X.485 was sent to all commands ordering that the existing Type A fuselage roundels should be converted into Type A.1 by the addition of an outer ring of Yellow of the same ring width as that of the existing rings. In addition, fin vertical stripes were to be carried, of the same width as the roundel rings, red forward.

These Dull Red, White and Dull Blue stripes varied considerably in style from squadron to squadron, and from aircraft type to type. A frequently-used style on operational Wellingtons at this time was the adoption of small stripes at the forward base of the fin, while those carried, for example, by the Wellingtons of 11 Operational Training Unit covered the entire fin. The smaller stripes on operational Wellingtons were probably used to make them less conspicuous, whereas the huge stripes on the training aircraft were to have the opposite effect. Blenheims, Whitleys and Hampdens usually had stripes covering the total height of the fin at this period, but of various widths. In many cases the stripes conformed to the laid-down rules, being of similar width to the rings of the fuselage roundels. In

Above right: A Blenheim IV, fresh from the Rootes production line, photographed at the end of April 1940. The photograph shows that the under-surfaces of Blenheims from the factories had been changed to Sky from the original Night paint. Note that the fuselage roundels are Type A. On May 1, the order was given to add a yellow outer ring to the fuselage roundels and to add fin stripes.

Right: Whitley V of 58 Squadron. Special Night (RDM2) paint had been extended up the fuselage sides and on the fins. The aircraft and squadron code letters are in grey, possibly Sky Grey in this case, The serial is in Dull Red. De-icing paste, dirty yellow in colour, is applied along the wing, tailplane and fin leading edges.

others, notably some Battles in France, the stripes covered the entire fin area in both height and width. Some Blenheims were similarly marked.

Various changes to the camouflage and markings of Service aircraft had been brought about since the outbreak of war by the sending of telegrams and signals: some of these communications were brief and open to wide interpretation, the signal relating to fin stripes being one example. In order to clarify the whole spectrum of camouflage and markings a conference was held at the Air Ministry on July 23, 1940, to try to standardise the subject as far as was possible. After the conference, on August 11, a directive was issued giving comprehensive details of the camouflage and markings to be carried by the various aircraft classes. One of the most important items to result from this conference was the adoption of a standard fin flash style in place of the many varied patterns in use after May 1. The new standard fin flash consisted of three stripes of Dull Red, white and Dull Blue, of 8in width, the overall rectangle being 27in high. The new fin flash was introduced as convenient over an extended period. It came into use on production lines quite quickly, but existing Service aircraft were repainted only when time permitted – such as during overhaul or repair. Thus it was some months before the new style stripes became the predominant form.

At this conference it was confirmed that the under surfaces of all operational aircraft should be painted in either Sky for day flying or Special Night for night flying. Even the wording used in the directive issued to squadrons after this conference still quoted popular descriptive names for colours – such as 'duck egg blue' for Sky and 'matt black' for Special Night. Another directive issued on September 6, 1940, clarified that 'matt black' meant Special Night on bombers.

As far as Bomber Command was concerned the Hampden, Wellington and Whitley were now used at night and therefore painted on their undersides with Special Night. The conference directive referred to Blenheim bombers and close support bombers, among other classes, as having Sky under surfaces, but at this period the Blenheim was virtually the only day bomber used by Bomber Command. A few Battles remained operational during this period but were operated at night and thus had night camouflage. The other important directive issued at this time was that roundels would not be carried under the wings of operational

Wellington ICs of 149 Squadron, September 1940. Special Night paint has been extended up the fuselage sides and on the fin. The serial has been painted around, leaving a camouflaged rectangle. When the order was given to extend the Special Night up the fuselage the fact that the serial numbers were already black had been overlooked. A further order, to paint the serials in Dull Red, was given on October 18, 1940. The white ring of the roundel has been washed over, possibly with weak black paint. Note the very small fin flash and the bad peeling of the Special Night paint where the rear gunner enters his turret.

aircraft, except fighters. Day or night bombers did not, therefore, carry roundels on their under surfaces after this date.

On September 4, 1940, a new order was issued to Bomber Command directing that the Special Night finish would be extended to cover the fins and rudders of bombers and that the Special Night finish would be extended up the fuselage sides for three quarters of the width. A number of squadrons after this directive introduced a wavy top line to the fuselage Special Night areas, possibly inspired by Handley Page's wavy demarcation line on Harrows and Hampdens before the war. This was the squadrons' own interpretation of the directive and quite unauthorised, which led eventually to correspondence within the Air Ministry and the eventual issue of a new directive ordering the top line of the fuselage Special Night to be straight. In the case of the Halifax – to quote just one example – the manufacturer's camouflage and markings drawings were accordingly revised on October 10, 1940.

When the Special Night finish was extended up the fuselage sides, no directive was issued to cover the painting of the rear fuselage serial numbers. This led to individual squadron interpretation: in some cases the serial letters and numerals were painted in Medium Sea Grey, while in others they were applied in Dull Red. On October 18, 1940, the Air Ministry clarified the situation by ordering the serial number to be painted in Dull Red.

The directive relating to the colour of the rear fuselage serial number was the last to be officially issued during 1940, but throughout the squadrons of Bomber Command there was disquiet about the conspicuousness of the national markings on the side of the fuselage and the fin or fins. While ready identification was very necessary over Britain during the hectic days of mid-1940, the same style of markings was too conspicuous and reflective in the vivid illumination of the searchlight web over Germany. Pending any official alteration in national markings squadrons started to adopt

measures to tone down the white, and in some cases the yellow rings in the fuselage roundels and the white bars in the fin stripes. A frequently used method during the latter part of 1940 was to paint over the entire roundel and fin flash white and Dull Red areas with thinned Medium Sea Grey. Being translucent this weak solution of Medium Sea Grey did not completely obliterate the white and Dull Red areas, but dulled them. At an earlier period some bombers, particularly Blenheims and Wellingtons, had been delivered from factories to aircraft storage units with large size Type A fuselage roundels. When it was ordered, on May 1, 1940, that an additional outer yellow ring should be added to the fuselage roundels, the large size of some of these factory-painted roundels only permitted the addition of a very narrow yellow ring. Aircraft with these roundels were commonly used during the second half of 1940, and the yellow rings, being narrow, were not as conspicuous as on the roundel of standard proportions, but the large white areas certainly required modification. As the year ended experimentation into lessening the reflectivity and brightness of the existing national markings continued. The operational experience and concern of the Bomber Command squadrons, shared by the night fighter crews who were also having serious problems in being too easily located by enemy bombers in a searchlight-illuminated area, led to official investigations into the problem by the Air Ministry and RAE. A further 18 months or so were to pass, however, before tests were completed and a new set of national markings was evolved and approved. In the meantime Bomber Command, and the night fighters, adopted their own methods to overcome the problem.

Whitley V of 78 Squadron, late 1940. Special Night paint up the fuselage sides and on the fins. Standard-size fin flashes. Code and aircraft letters in Medium Sea Grey. Serials in Dull Red. White of roundels and fin flashes over-painted with Medium Sea Grey.